"Personal peace is key to living a renewing life. *Ripples of Peace* offers a thought-provoking array of resources and simple ideas for practicing and cultivating peace in your life and the world. Reading this book evokes calm and serenity."

– **Krista Kurth**, Ph.D. and **Suzanne Adele Schmidt**, Ph.D., co-authors of
Running on Plenty at Work: Renewal Strategies for Individuals

"At no time has the need for visionary and compassionate living been more apparent. Rae Thompson has crafted a generous resource of practices and references that gently challenge and encourage us to talk, write, share, think about and, most importantly, *be* peace."

– **Ann Kline**, spiritual director, program coordinator for group spiritual direction,
Shalem Institute for Spiritual Formation, and contributing author to
"The Lived Experience of Group Spiritual Direction"

"*Ripples of Peace* is a true gift from the heart. Through her pearls, pictures, and prayers, Rae Thompson teaches all of us that peace starts from inside. If we are to build one healthy global society then we must first discover the peace within us and share it with our families, friends, and the world. What a beautifully written and precious book."

– **Bob Rosen**, CEO of Healthy Companies International and author of
Global Literacies, Leading People, and *The Healthy Company*

"For peacemakers of all ages, Rae has given us an illuminating guide for practical application of our beliefs and hopes for a world in which personal and planetary peace is not only possible, but a natural outgrowth of our human evolution."

– **James Durst**, singer/songwriter, WorldWind recording artist

"*Ripples of Peace* is a rich gift. It combines a deep call to the soul with practical suggestions and resources for realizing peace. The book invites learning by providing the framework for meaningful experimentation, reflection, and creative expression—for individuals and groups of all ages."

– **Michael Milano**, author of *Designing Powerful Training*, consultant in training and
organizational development, and adjunct faculty at Georgetown University

"*Ripples of Peace* is an inspiration for everyone, every day. The philosophy is sound, the principles are true, and *peace* is the ultimate result."

— **Michelle Lusson**, D.D., author of *Creative Wellness* and president, Creative Wellness, Inc.

"Rae Thompson writes with insight, intelligence and clarity. Her sincere commitment shines through on every page. The quotes from sages, authors, teachers, great peacemakers, and scriptures add a timeless wisdom and depth to the author's admonitions. Anyone walking the path of peace will find a valuable guide and a helping hand along the way in *Ripples of Peace*."

— **Stephen Longfellow Fiske**, singer/songwriter and author of *The Art of Peace*

"*Ripples of Peace* draws you into contemplation and quiet action using the most unassuming, yet powerful, activities. You have the option of *doing* something for peace or *being* peaceful; the opportunities for both are fully present and quietly provocative. Your creativity grows and, with it, your efforts for peace."

— **Judith H. LaRosa**, Ph.D., R.N., Deputy Director, Master of Public Health Program, Department of Preventive Medicine and Community Health, SUNY Downstate Medical Center

"The Spirit of Peace is a living presence, vast and powerful beyond anything we have yet imagined. *Ripples of Peace* is generously poetic; it opens a door in our imaginations through which we can touch this vast Spirit and let it touch us. Focusing my attention on *Ripples of Peace* has helped me create a more peaceful personal world. And I have found that reading sections of the book out loud is a potent technique for generating and sustaining a strong and lasting sense of peace."

— **Carolann Heckman**, poet and writer

"Rae provided invaluable assistance to me in writing about my spiritual journey. Now, her book on peace continues to give me her wise counsel. Words evoke visuals, visuals evoke words—what a treat to have this splendid combination in an exploration of the most significant topic of our time."

— **Liz Clist**, writer and speaker on issues of the spirit

Ripples of Peace

111 Ways You Can Help Create Peace in the World

RAE THOMPSON

Heartswork Publications
Reston, VA

Published by Heartswork Publications
A Division of Heartswork
2169 Glencourse Lane
Reston, VA 20191 USA
www.hearts-work.com

ISBN 0-9743094-0-0
LCCN 2003109607

Cover photograph and all interior photographs (except author's portrait)
© Mark Tucker, Healing Heart Productions

For information regarding special discounts for bulk purchases, please contact
Heartswork Publications at 703-648-1464, *heartswork@comcast.net*, or
www.ripples-of-peace.com.

This book is dedicated to everyone whose life was touched by the tragic events of September 11, 2001:

> To those who died and those who live
>
> To those who take and those who give
>
> To those who scorn and those who cheer
>
> To all who love and all who fear.

May it help us remember that whatever we do unto others, in truth, we do to ourselves, for *we are one*.

Contents

Foreword

You can help create peace in the world. That is the premise—and the subtitle—of this book. In fact, the author gives you 111 practical suggestions for how you can do this. She provides you with inspiring quotes, beautiful photographs, and useful resources to help you. Now I want to talk about why it is imperative that you accept this challenge and this opportunity.

Rae Thompson wrote this book as a way of taking personal responsibility for changing the world after September 11. On that day, many of us made or renewed our commitments to work for peace, justice, and understanding among the many peoples who share this planet. We saw, in vivid Technicolor, the inevitable results of living in a culture of separation, where it's "us against them," where imposing one's will on another is accepted as "how things are," and where violence is both a tool of and a response to that domination.

We saw too that our leaders would stay on the war path, ensuring that the cycles of revenge and retaliation would only escalate. We saw that few, if any, were able to articulate either an understanding of how such an event could occur, or a vision of how to build a world where terrorist acts of this nature would be unlikely. In short, we saw a response that dealt with symptoms, not with causes.

The underlying foundation of this book, and of all my work in the world, is that there is another way, a better way. Wherever I speak about peace, people always ask me, "But don't you think we human beings are wired for violence, that wars and aggression are basic to human nature, and that therefore peace is an idealistic and unrealistic dream?" My response is that yes, violence and aggression seem to be a common part of the human experience, but they are not the only things that define us.

We also have inherently within us the template for Peace, for Justice, for Freedom, for Equality, for Harmony—all these words that start with capital letters because they represent the highest goals of humanity. We have the capacity to destroy life or to support and honor life, to see ourselves as separate or as one, to live in fear or in love. We can choose the familiar path of violence, or we can choose the less familiar path of peace. The point is, *we can choose.*

Not only can we choose, but world events are waking us up to the reality that *we must choose.* The human family stands at a critical choice point. We have developed weapons and lifestyles that can destroy all life on this planet. If we continue to live as we have, and to engage others in the world in the manner to which we are accustomed, we will surely arrive at a point where someone, somewhere, will use those weapons. Or, we can take another road, the peace path, and create a new way of being together on this one planet we all call home.

Our souls hunger for peace; our hearts tell us it is possible; our minds search eagerly for ways to make it so. This is our human destiny, our evolutionary assignment—to create peace on earth. We already know much of what this path can look like: We will realize that there is only one of us, that, as Mother Theresa says, "we belong to each other," and treat each other accordingly. We will engage in dialogue, develop mutual understanding, solve conflicts nonviolently, and see our diversity as gifts enhancing all. We will realize that as one suffers, we all suffer, so we will use the vast resources of this planet to ensure the basic needs of all its inhabitants. We will live in harmony with the natural world. We will, as the Navajo people say, "walk in beauty."

September 11 reminded us, quite rudely, that this is the goal, a goal that can be accomplished only if each one of us stands up and takes respon–sibility for acting, in our own lives, to turn that potential into reality. The particular action is less important than the intention and the commit–ment to act. There are infinite things each one of us can do, whoever we are and however we live, to generate more peace in our lives and in the world. Every small step matters; each one makes the path a little bit wider and a little bit more inviting for others. This book presents 111 suggestions for such personal action. Taken one by one, they can change your life. Taken together, they can change the world.

Once September 11 happened, we all had a job to do. Rae Thompson did hers, and did it with grace and beauty. Now it's time for you, dear reader, to do yours.

Louise Diamond, Ph.D.

Author of *The Peace Book: 108 Simple Ways to Create a More Peaceful World* and *The Courage for Peace*; president, The Peace Company

Introduction

On September 11, 2001, I was working alone in my Virginia office as the twin towers in New York City crumpled to the ground and sections of the Pentagon collapsed in crimson flames. I was sublimely unaware of the devastation and destruction that, over the next few days, would be indelibly imprinted onto our national psyche. Around 3:00 PM, after hearing the astonishing news from a friend, I found myself both mesmerized and repelled by the televised images of the terrorist attacks. For the first time in my life, I felt afraid to be an American in my own country, my own home.

Glued to the television set over the ensuing week, I absorbed story after story about lost loved ones, improbable rescues, and profound heroism. I learned of the elaborate planning that had taken place to orchestrate the day of terror and took to heart the warnings of additional attacks. I heard President Bush outline his plan to declare war on terrorism and to protect Americans at home.

My disbelief and dismay soon gave way to a series of questions: Could bombs and bullets bring about a real peace? Could actions born of fear and anger lead to the mutual respect and reverence for life that are requisites for peace? What could the United States and other countries do to address the conditions underlying terrorism and, in so doing, foster a lasting peace? How could young people who had experienced only war be helped to envision and embrace peace? And, more practically, what could *I* do to help create such a peace?

I quickly realized that the first four questions were best debated by scholars, philosophers, politicians, journalists, and others who possessed a comprehensive understanding of these complex issues. The last question, however, was one I was willing and eager to tackle.

Ripples of Peace: 111 Ways You Can Help Create Peace in the World is the result of my quest for answers. It is a synthesis of my research, personal exploration, and intimate conversations with friends. Far from being comprehensive, the 111 ways described in the book provide many possible first steps on a lifelong journey of peace. I offer them as possibilities to anyone choosing to help replace the fear, despair, hatred, and terror felt by so many people around the globe with faith, joy, love, and peace—one person and one day at a time.

About the Book

Ripples of Peace consists of two parts. Part One describes 111 things you can do to nurture and sustain peace, first within yourself and then with your family, friends, community, nation, and the world. The explanation of each item is specific enough for you to take action and general enough for you to be flexible and innovative with what you choose to do. Part Two contains information to help you expand and deepen your peacefulness, including peace prayers from around the world, meditations, an imagination session on peace, recommended books and magazines, and dozens of peace-related organizations. You can find additional resources at local libraries and book stores, as well as on the Internet.

Although the items in Part One are divided into three sections, you will find that you can adapt many of the items in one section for use in another section. For example, even though "Be generous" appears in the section on creating inner peace, it can also contribute to peace among your family and friends, as well as in your community, nation, and the world. And "Listen attentively with an open mind and heart," found in the section on family and friends, is equally applicable to your relationships with all the people in your life.

We must be the change we wish to see in the world.

– Mohandas K. Gandhi

Peace is not a relationship of nations.
It is a condition of mind brought about
by a serenity of soul…
Lasting peace can come only to peaceful people.

– Jawaharlal Nehru

Many of the 111 ways to help create peace are straightforward and easy to do in a short period of time. Some require more time and attention. Quite a few are repeatable single events, while others are most meaningful when made an integral part of your life. And, even though the majority of the 111 ways involve some form of activity, a considerable number require a fundamental shift in consciousness, a new way of thinking about and responding to the world. It is this embodiment of peace as a *way of being* that makes the *ways of doing* so effective in creating peace within ourselves and with others.

Taken together, the 111 suggestions in this book reflect an overall approach to peace, one that is based on a reverence for life and the belief that, because we are all connected, the actions of one of us has the potential to affect all of us. The book is, in essence, a tribute to the power of one. As each one of us dwells within peace, we automatically radiate peace to those around us who, in turn, pass peace along, like ripples in a pond.

If we are interdependent with everything and everyone,

even our smallest, least significant thought, word,

and action have real consequences throughout the universe.

Throw a pebble into a pond. It sends a shiver across

the surface of the water. Ripples merge into one another

and create new ones. Everything is inextricably interrelated:

We come to realize that we are responsible for everything

we do, say, or think, responsible in fact for ourselves,

everyone and everything else, and the entire universe.

– Sogyal Rinpoche

A Special Note

As you read this book, feel free to experiment with those items to which you are drawn. In addition, pay close attention to items that require you to stretch beyond the familiar, for they may be the ones from which you derive the greatest benefit. If many of these ideas are new to you, explore those you find most appealing to discover the ones that work best for you. If you have already incorporated a lot of the ways of being and doing into your life, use the book for inspiration or as a checklist to keep yourself on track. In either case, use your creativity to expand these ideas or develop your own activities for inner and outer peace.

PART ONE

Cultivating Peace

If there is to be peace in the world,

There must be peace in the nations.

If there is to be peace in the nations,

There must be peace in the cities.

If there is to be peace in the cities,

There must be peace between neighbors.

If there is to be peace between neighbors,

There must be peace in the home.

If there is to be peace in the home,

There must be peace in the heart.

– Lao-Tsu

Creating Peace within Yourself

Peace begins with you.

The most important single thing any of us can do to help create peace in the world around us is to create and sustain peace within ourselves. This is indeed fortunate since each one of us is the *only* person whose life we can *truly change*. Once we are peaceful within, we are poised to help foster and promote peace among our families and friends, in our communities and countries, and around the world.

Inner peace, as presented in this book, refers to our pervading sense of contentment and well–being, along with our awareness that all is well. It most frequently involves feelings of calmness and serenity, as well as freedom from negative thoughts and emotions. Inner peace is often characterized by our sense of oneness with the divine or our deep love and compassion for others. It is sometimes linked to actions that are fully aligned with our true selves. At times, inner peace is accompanied by considerable energy and our genuine enthusiasm for being in the universal flow of life.

The cultivation of inner peace is a lifelong process. It involves making choices and taking actions consistent with peace on a day–by–day and, occasionally, a minute–by–minute basis. As such, the experience of inner peace is a journey, rather than a destination, requiring occasional re-routes, reversals, and recommitments.

To help create and sustain peace within yourself, select from the following pages those actions that appeal to you. Start with items that are familiar to you and then experiment with some that are new. Feel free to borrow items from the other two sections and to create your own inner peace-making activities. When you find actions that bring you deep and abiding peace, make them an integral part of your life.

1

Write about what peace means to you

Knowing where we are going is necessary if we are to reach a desired destination. In much the same way, being familiar with what inner peace means to us can be instrumental in helping us attain such peace.

Focus on what it would be like for you if there were peace in your life, your family, your community, your country, and the world. Describe your life as you think it would be in the midst of peace.

Write in the present tense, starting with "I am..." or "I have..."

Avoid writing about what is missing (no more war, terrorism, or poverty) and concentrate on what is actually *present* (peace, safety, and abundance). Be specific about where you are, what you are doing, and what you see and hear.

When your written image is clear, focus on your feelings of inner peace and ask yourself the following question:

- What does it *feel* like to have peace in my life, to be fully and completely at peace?

Review and update your written picture of peace periodically, as you increase your awareness and understanding of what peace means to you.

Recall and deepen your feelings of peace often.

4

2

Draw a picture of peace

Drawing a picture of peace allows us to communicate what is in our hearts, free from the complications of thoughts and words. It can also expand our understanding of what peace means to us.

Sit in a quiet place for five to ten minutes and allow yourself to relax and feel peaceful. Play soothing music in the background if you like. When you feel completely at ease, use crayons, paints, or markers to draw a picture of peace on paper or artist's canvas.

5

Allow your hand to create the picture without a lot of input from your inner critic. Try using your nondominant hand to help bring out your creative spirit.

Consider framing your picture and placing it where you will see it every day.

3

Find and display quotations about peace

Surrounding ourselves with reminders of peace is a wonderful way to keep us focused on our commitment to creating peace in our lives.

Look on the Internet and through magazines, newspapers, and books for sayings, prayers, and quotations about peace from individuals you admire. Cut out or copy the quotations and put them on your refrigerator, mirror, or other place where you will see them often.

You may find that repeating your favorite quotation, along with your daily prayers, or at times when you begin to feel anger or fear, helps you maintain your inner peace.

4

Pray for peace and then live as if your prayer has been answered

Asking for divine assistance in the pursuit of peace is a natural and important human activity. Prayers for peace, such as those found in Part Two, are common in all spiritual traditions.

After making a heartfelt request for peace in your life or in the world, allow yourself to believe your prayer is being answered affirmatively. Then live in the faith that your request is granted, even when there is no evidence that this is so.

In future prayers, give thanks for God's answer to your plea. By expressing gratitude for peace already given, you confirm your trust in divine action.

Consider making the giving of thanks for peace an integral part of your daily prayers.

*There are many things that are essential to arriving at true
peace of mind, and one of the most important is faith,
which cannot be acquired without prayer.*

– John Wooden

*Gratitude unlocks the fullness of life. It turns what we have
into enough, and more. It turns denial into acceptance, chaos
into order, confusion to clarity…It turns problems into gifts,
failures into successes, the unexpected into perfect timing, and
mistakes into important events…Gratitude makes sense of our
past, brings peace for today, and creates a vision for tomorrow.*

– Melodie Beattie

5

Enjoy nature

Many people feel a connection with all of creation while enjoying time in natural settings. Walking in the woods, watching the sun rise or set, and inhaling the sweet fragrance of fresh flowers can enhance our feelings of peace and joy. Observing animals at play or birds in flight, listening to the wind, gazing at the stars, and feeling the coolness of rain or snow on our faces can nourish our souls and replace our tensions and anxieties with a sense of well-being.

Find time to commune with nature and to contemplate nature's beauty. Make it a habit.

Consider bringing nature indoors. Adorn your home and office with flowers, houseplants, or potted herbs to enhance your sense of well-being and peacefulness.

10

6

Use photographs and artwork to enhance peaceful feelings

Images often speak to us more powerfully than words. Many people find that photographs and paintings of natural settings, as well as pictures of loved ones and pets, evoke feelings of love, contentment, and peace.

Surround yourself at home and at work with photographs and other artwork that engender feelings of serenity. Display pictures of places that have special meaning to you, sacred sites you have visited or are drawn to, and the people and animals you love. Focus on these images often, especially when you start to feel tense or stressed, to help preserve your inner peace.

11

7

Maintain a clutter-free environment

The ancient Eastern art of Feng Shui asserts that the unimpeded flow of energy within a room or house can heighten feelings of well–being. Clutter, which often represents activities left undone or items hoarded for some unforeseen time, can interfere with the clear state of mind in which peacefulness thrives.

12

Clean out your desk, files, closets, storage room, attic, basement, and garage. Keep only what you actually use and store keepsakes away in an accessible place. Donate the remaining items to charity or give them to friends and family members who have an immediate use for them.

Repeat this process annually to create peace both within and around you.

8

Think *from* peace

There is evidence that we subconsciously draw to ourselves those experiences that are in sync with our recurring thoughts. Therefore, by focusing our attention on what we find peaceful, we can reinforce our inner peace and calm.

Pay attention to your thoughts. Learn to replace nonpeaceful ones with thoughts that bring you peace and a sense of well-being.

To take this notion a step further, experiment with the *way* you focus on peacefulness. Instead of thinking *about* being peaceful, which implies that you and peace are separate, think *from* peacefulness, as if it were already present within you.

For example, if you find yourself worrying about a future event, begin instead to concentrate on the event running smoothly and how you feel when it is successfully completed. Go beyond thinking that you *will* be peaceful to believing that you already *are* peaceful. Put yourself in the mind-set of currently experiencing the peaceful outcome of the event. Then act as if this were true.

The more often you practice thinking *from* peace, the faster and easier it becomes.

13

What we are today comes from our thoughts of yesterday,
and our present thoughts build our life of tomorrow:
Our life is the creation of our mind.

– The Buddha

You know a thing mentally by looking at it from the outside,
by comparing it with other things, by analyzing it and
defining it; (by thinking of it): whereas you can know a
thing spiritually only by becoming it, (only by thinking
from it). You must be the thing itself and not merely talk
about it or look at it.

– Neville

9

Enjoy time with a loving animal

The unconditional love offered by a pet or other loving animal is a wonderful source of joy and contentment. Petting a dog or cat has even been shown to lower blood pressure and decrease anxiety.

Make time to connect with your pet, if you already have one, or consider getting one if you choose to give yourself such a gift. Or enjoy the pet of a friend or family member whenever you can.

16

10

Listen to music that exemplifies peace to you

Music can affect mood. It can inspire our creativity, enhance our well-being, increase our energy, and uplift our spirits. It can also help us relax. Some music even speaks to our hearts or stirs our souls, reminding us of our reflection of the divine.

Make it a habit to play music that instills peace—at home, at work, and in your car. And remember to use music regularly to maintain your positive mood.

Be mindful of the lyrics of music you listen to regularly. Words that affirm love, peace, and joy contribute to your experience of peacefulness.

17

11

Read what inspires you and brings you peace

Many of us find inspiration in the words and stories of others.

Seek out articles and books that uplift you and bring you peace. Find religious and inspirational texts that speak to you. Subscribe to newsletters and magazines that focus on hope, spirituality, joy, and love.

Consider setting aside a specific time each day to read something that deepens your inner peace.

18

12

Make a list of what and whom you feel anger toward and then resolve each item, one at a time

Recognizing and expressing anger in healthy ways is essential to maintain our integrity and the quality of our relationships. Each time we allow ourselves to hold on to anger or bury it, we interfere with our inner peace. To extend and expand our peacefulness, we can either resolve what angers us or find ways to transform our anger into its antidote, forgiveness.

Make a list of all the people and circumstances about which you feel anger. Be honest. Include everyone and everything. Then address each item on your list, as you feel ready, by either taking steps to make peace with the person or circumstance or by cultivating forgiveness and peace within yourself through prayer, meditation, or other means.

When you no longer feel anger related to a specific item on your list, cross it off. Be patient with yourself: this process may take some time.

19

As we come to balance in our lives, our anger will diminish.
If we develop a sense of spirituality, choose loving friends, learn
skills for intimacy, speak our truths, and develop compassion,
there will be fewer occasions that trigger anger…
While we may feel angry, it won't separate us from
wisdom or the ability to be thoughtful.

– Charlotte Kasl

20

Creating Peace within Yourself

13

Call a friend to help restore your inner peace

Occasionally we may feel upset enough by a situation or person that the things we normally do to restore our peacefulness fail to work for us. These are the times that contacting a good friend can help us regain a perspective that brings us back to peace.

The next time you find yourself unable to reclaim your inner peace, call a friend you know will lovingly listen to you and offer you caring support and kindness. Talk briefly about what is on your mind and then ask your friend to help you reconnect with your heart.

14

Burn incense

The burning of incense to calm and uplift the human spirit has been practiced by many people throughout recorded history. It is especially common among people of Eastern faiths.

Incense comes in a variety of forms and fragrances and can be found in stores and through on-line sources that specialize in products related to New Age topics and Eastern spiritual traditions.

23

Find a fragrance that appeals to you and make the burning of incense an integral part of your prayers or meditation practice. Or use it in your home at regular intervals for its calming effect.

15

Add a water feature to your home or office

Water is often associated with emotions. Trickling water and serene lakes are considered soothing, while ocean waves and hard rain can feel quite intense.

Place an indoor water fountain in your home or at work to add a calming effect to any room. Install an outdoor water feature to soften traffic noises or provide a sense of peacefulness to your garden or entry way.

Make sure that the water remains clear and in motion.

24

16

Explore fear, anger, and despair to find faith, forgiveness, and joy

Fear and faith, anger and forgiveness, and despair and joy are opposites. It is impossible for any of these opposing feelings to coexist within us in the same moment.

As you become aware of fear, anger, or despair, you can use your aware-ness to open the door to faith, forgiveness, or joy. First, note and acknowledge exactly what you are feeling, without resisting or repressing it. Second, ask yourself whether you choose to hold on to this feeling or to transform it into its opposite. If you choose transformation, do what-ever it takes to move yourself into faith, forgiveness, and joy.

For example, you might recite affirmations, say a prayer, listen to soothing music, play with your children or a pet, or meditate. The instant you allow in feelings of love and peace, you begin to tip the scale: from fear toward faith, from anger toward forgiveness, and from despair toward joy.

As you practice transforming your feelings in this manner, you are likely to notice that the shifts occur faster and last longer.

Moving beyond fear may be the single most important thing that you can do for yourself. And your planet.

– Sharif Abdullah

When, as individuals, we disarm ourselves internally—through countering our negative thoughts and emotions and cultivating positive qualities—we create the conditions for external disarmament. Indeed, genuine, lasting world peace will only be possible as a result of each of us making an effort internally.

– The Dalai Lama

Violence has its roots in every heart. It is in my own heart that I must recognize fear, agitation, coldness, alienation, and the impulse to blind anger. Here in my heart I can turn fear into courageous trust, agitation and confusion into stillness, isolation into a sense of belonging, alienation into love, and irrational reaction into common sense.

– Brother David Steindl-Rast

Creating Peace within Yourself

17

Follow the energy and flow of life

Noticing what we are doing when time seems to pass by quickly reveals the activities that feed our souls. Being alert to fluctuations in our levels of enthusiasm for various tasks and people gives us clues to our hearts' desires. Responding to these promptings from our souls and hearts can lead us to an inner peace based on the clear and creative expression of our authentic selves.

Pay attention to your levels of energy and enthusiasm. Then follow the energy by making choices that allow you to

- engage in activities that give you energy

- be with people who enhance your sense of happiness and peace

- express your true self.

As you do these things, you may begin to feel that you have stepped into the natural flow of life and are strengthening your connection to the divine.

18

Visit web sites related to peace

The Internet is replete with information related to peace. It offers vast resources for creating inner peace and for helping to create peace within your family, community, nation, and the world.

Explore the Web's resources to learn more about the suggestions in this book and to make connections with others of like mind and heart. Consider registering at selected sites to receive updates on what others are doing to promote peace around the planet.

19

Recite affirmations of peace

An affirmation is a statement that clearly and directly expresses what we desire. It may affirm something that we believe or something that we choose to have, to do, or to be. By repeatedly stating what we desire in the present tense, as if it were already true, we condition our subconscious mind to accept it as fact.

Select a peace affirmation from the list below or create one of your own. Recite it out loud as often as possible, perhaps adding it to your daily prayers or meditation. Say the affirmation quietly to yourself whenever you experience feelings that interfere with your inner peace.

Examples of peace affirmations:

- I am peace.

- I am relaxed and at peace.

- I am an instrument of divine peace.

- I fully embody peace in this and every moment.

- My body and mind are filled with divine peace.

- I am secure in the peace of God.

- I maintain the presence of peace within myself at all times.

20

Meditate daily

The primary purpose of most types of meditation is to gain access to a higher level of consciousness. Some people describe meditation as a means of experiencing oneness with God or the Universe. Others talk about meditation as a way to calm the mind and attain an awareness of serenity, clarity, and bliss.

There are numerous meditation traditions and dozens of meditation techniques, the majority of which involve concentrating on an object, a sound or word (mantra), or your breath. Regular meditation practice can enhance your ability to relax, increase your awareness, foster mental focus and clarity, and generate a pervading sense of peace within you, both during and after your session.

Look into the meditation courses and centers in your area and select a meditation method that feels right for you. Sign up for a class or find a book that tells you what to do. Or go on–line to investigate your options.

31

The practice of meditation is not the source of the peace we feel,
it reveals the peace that is already within us.

– Robert Rabbin

Peace comes within the souls of men
When they realize their oneness with the universe.

– Black Elk

21

Lighten up

When we are intensely serious about ourselves and everything we do, it is possible to overreact to situations and to override our inner peace. The process of loosening and lightening up often gives us new insights on how to solve problems, move forward with an important project, and reconnect with what is meaningful in our lives.

34

If your life feels like a burden, it may be time to lighten the load.

Find something light-hearted to do. Go out with friends, watch a funny movie, read a whimsical book, or make a play date with your children. Look through this book for other suggestions that can help you feel lighter.

22

Sing songs of peace

Music is the language of the heart. The heart, in turn, is where peace resides.

Allow your heart to sing of peace. You can do this by singing others' songs of peace or by writing and singing your own songs.

Sing in the shower, while driving your car, or when doing the dishes or other routine activities. The repetition of the words and music serves to reinforce your experience of peace.

Remember to sing wholeheartedly.

23

Write a poem of peace

Poetry gives voice to the soul. It seems to emanate from deep within us. Poetry can bypass our busy minds and express the simple truths known only to our hearts and souls.

Put aside any doubts you may have about your prowess as a poet and write a poem of peace. Keep it simple, as though you were writing it for a ten–year–old child.

Consider sharing your poem with your family and friends. You may even choose to add it to birthday or holiday cards.

24

Practice nonattachment

Change may well be the only constant in the world. Nothing stays exactly the same for any length of time. Remaining attached to the "way things are" is an invitation to disappointment and unnecessary suffering.

Notice how life changes around and within you. Pay attention to how the people in your life change over time and how nature alters itself through the seasons. Think about how your house and the items in it, your work, and your children have changed and are changing. Be aware of how you feel different from day to day, sometimes from minute to minute.

Practice letting go of any attachment you may have to people and things as they currently are. Allow yourself to peacefully and lovingly accept impermanence as a natural part of life.

As you improve your ability to remain detached from the way your life is at any given moment, you are likely to discover that you experience less stress. You may, instead, find yourself increasingly peaceful.

He who binds to himself a Joy,

Does the winged life destroy;

He who kisses the Joy as it flies,

Lives in Eternity's sunrise.

– William Blake

Creating Peace within Yourself

25

Use audio and video tapes to deepen your inner peace

Listening to what experienced teachers and professionals have to say on topics related to peace can confirm and expand our own ideas. Their perspectives may trigger new insights about how we might attain inner peace or add new images to our personal pictures of peace in the world.

40

Find and listen to audio tapes or watch video tapes that contain inspiring messages from people you admire on subjects that have meaning to you. Select those that offer ways to enrich your inner peace.

26

Make contact with Mother Earth

There is something extraordinarily rejuvenating, perhaps magical, about touching the earth. It calls forth the playful child within us and offers us a chance to be one with life itself, to remember our peaceful connection with all that is. This is true whether we make contact with our hands, bare feet, or full bodies.

Take advantage of opportunities to dig in the dirt or sand. Plant flowers, build a sand castle, or make friends with a rock. Take off your shoes and socks and wiggle your toes in the grass or the sand. Climb a tree or swim in a natural body of water such as a pond, lake, river, or the ocean.

Immerse yourself in these activities. Feel the pulse of Mother Earth. Imagine that you are sending your energy into the ground or water, while the source of all life sends divine energy into your body through the palms of your hands or the soles of your feet.

41

27

Practice yoga

The ancient practice of yoga has many forms and types. Perhaps the most well-known type in this country is Hatha yoga, which involves body poses (asanas) and breathing techniques intended to induce relaxation and a state of silent awareness, free from tension and stress. Because of its focus, the regular practice of yoga becomes an invitation to peace.

42

Attend or observe classes in the different types of yoga available in your area to determine the one that best suits you and that amplifies your inner peace. Once you have identified your preferred style of yoga, sign up for classes or purchase a tape or book to guide you in doing yoga at home.

28

Learn to be at home in silence

Most of us are accustomed to having a lot of noise in our lives. Although we often say we long for peace and quiet, we may still find ourselves uncomfortable with long periods of silence.

How often have you spoken up to break a lull in a conversation? How many times have you turned on the radio or television for background noise or to avoid being alone? How frequently have you allowed your internal thoughts to disrupt your peace of mind?

Peace gains strength in silence. Cultivate your ability to enjoy and nurture the silence in your life.

43

To make possible true inner silence, practice:

Silence of the eyes, by seeking always the beauty and goodness of God everywhere, closing them to the faults of others and to all that is sinful and disturbing to the soul;

Silence of the ears, by listening always to the voice of God and to the cry of the poor and the needy, closing them to all other voices that come from all human nature, such as gossip, tale-bearing, and uncharitable words;

Silence of the tongue, by praising God and speaking the life-giving word of God that is the Truth, that enlightens and inspires, brings peace, hope, and joy, and by refraining from self-defense and every word that causes darkness, turmoil, pain, and death;

Silence of the mind, by opening it to the truth and knowledge of God in prayer and contemplation…;

Silence of the heart, by loving God with our heart, soul, mind, and strength and one another as God loves, and avoiding all selfishness, hatred, envy, jealousy, and greed.

– Mother Teresa

Creating Peace within Yourself

29

Be attentive to your body's messages

Our bodies are storehouses of thoughts and feelings. They send us messages that can help us maintain our peacefulness.

Pay attention to what your body tells you. Notice how your body reacts when you are tense or anxious and how it feels when you are calm and serene.

Chances are that feelings of anger, frustration, and fear cause your muscles to tighten, your head to hurt, or your stomach to churn. Your whole body may seem tense or tightened. These feelings of contraction may precede full-blown thoughts of anger, fear, or other emotions that can disrupt your inner peace.

As you become aware of subtle tensions in your body, you can experiment with ways to release that tightness and to relax. You might take a walk, go swimming, meditate, get a massage, practice yoga, or listen to soothing music. You might purposefully alternate contracting and relaxing the major muscles in your body until you feel at ease.

Practice interpreting and responding to your body's signals to sustain your sense of contentment and peace.

30

Play with young children

Anytime we connect with the playfulness of a child, or see the world through a child's delight, we open a channel to peacefulness. In addition, our willingness to meet a child on his or her terms serves to strengthen that child's sense of safety and well-being.

Make time to play with children. Ask them what they like to do. Allow the child within you to surface. Tell stories. Invent new games. Be silly. Roll in the grass. Color, paint, or draw. Sing goofy songs. Laugh.

Notice how fast the time flies.

31

Become involved in a religious or spiritual community that speaks to your heart

The communion of spirit that occurs in a religious or spiritual setting can enliven our personal sense of peace. The more aligned we are with the philosophy and practices of the group, the greater the benefits.

Find a community, however large or small, traditional or new, with which you feel a heart connection. Attend meetings or services and take part in group activities on a regular basis.

32

Cultivate compassion

The road to peace is paved with compassion.

Compassion is often seen, as it is in the Buddhist tradition, as more than a sense of sympathy or the recognition of another person's suffering; it encompasses a sustained commitment to help alleviate that suffering. True compassion requires that we allow ourselves to feel the pain of others without shutting down our minds or closing our hearts to them.

Cultivate compassion within yourself for the people in your life and throughout the world. Open your heart. Practice seeing through the eyes of another.

Remember to be compassionate toward yourself as well.

49

We can begin right now to practice calming our anger, looking deeply at the roots of the hatred and violence in our society and in our world, and listening with compassion in order to hear and understand what we have not yet had the capacity to hear and to understand…When we have listened and looked deeply, we may begin to develop the energy of brotherhood and sisterhood between all nations, which is the deepest spiritual heritage of all religious and cultural traditions. In this way, the peace and understanding within the whole world is increased day by day.

– Thich Nhat Hahn

Until he extends his circle of compassion to include all living things, man will not himself find peace.

– Albert Schweitzer

Creating Peace within Yourself

33

Create a peace theme for each year

It is common practice to set goals for ourselves at the beginning of a new year. Unfortunately, many of us abandon these goals within one or two months.

Instead of establishing goals this year, consider creating a theme for yourself that relates to peace. A theme gives you a solid framework for your choices and actions throughout the year, while being flexible enough to accommodate occasional slips.

Pick one theme for the entire year. Cultivating inner peace, being more compassionate with others, and participating in events or organizations for peace are excellent peace themes.

Consider expanding your theme by creating a specific activity for each month. If your theme is to cultivate inner peace, for example, you might begin to read inspirational books in January, start meditating in February, add walks in nature to your routine in March, and so forth.

Post your theme where you will see it every day and be patient and gentle with yourself as you go through the year. If you miss an opportunity to act on your theme, just reaffirm your commitment for the next time.

34

Explore various forms of bodywork and movement

Tensions accumulate in the body. Plus, many of us unknowingly hold our bodies in certain postures that may help us suppress deep feelings or reinforce self-limiting thoughts. Bodywork and certain forms of movement can help us relax, enhance the flow of energy throughout our bodies, and open the door to a new freedom of expression and peace. They may even aid in healing certain physical and emotional ailments that interfere with our feelings of contentment and ease.

Examples of bodywork include many forms of massage, the Alexander Technique, Hellerwork, Tragerwork, the Feldenkrais Method, rolfing and reflexology, acupressure, therapeutic touch, and polarity therapy. Examples of movement include dance, Eurythmy, the Continuum, Tai Chi, and Qigong.

Find out what is available in your area and explore the types of body-work or movement that appeal to you. If you find yourself strongly drawn to a particular form of bodywork or movement, consider taking a course or getting certified as a practitioner.

53

35

Create sacred space in your home

The space in our homes conducts both light and energy and can detract from or add to our sense of peace. By creating sacred areas within our living environment, we can maximize the positive effects of our outer space on our inner space.

Identify an area within your home that you choose to designate as your sacred space, a place where you can get away from busy-ness and stress to find inner safety and peace. Imbue that area with love and harmony by declaring your intention for its use. Then arrange the space to suit its purpose, including a place to sit or meditate, an altar, or whatever comforts you. Burn incense and candles in your space to help create a peaceful atmosphere.

Use your sacred space daily to practice spiritual rituals, pray, meditate, read uplifting books, or listen to peaceful music. Notice how the peace from your sacred space begins to permeate the rest of your house.

36

Imagine peace before you fall asleep each night

Most of us are intimately familiar with the problems and conflicts in our lives and in the world. By using our imaginations each night before we go to sleep, we can become increasingly familiar with what it is like to live in peace. And the more we know what it feels like to be peaceful, the more easily we can access our inner peace whenever we choose.

Right before you drift off to sleep, imagine what your life is like when specific conflicts are resolved, and when peace pervades your life. Put yourself in the picture of your mind's eye. Make it real.

- What does the sensation of peace feel like?

- Where are you and what are you doing?

- What do you hear, see, smell, touch, and taste?

- Who is with you?

- What do you feel?

- What is different in your life?

Feel grateful for your imagined peace as you fall asleep.

Repeat this exercise each night, carry the peaceful feelings with you throughout each day, act as if peace prevails, and notice how your life begins to change.

55

*The possibility of life is inherent within the capacity to imagine
what life is, backed by the power to produce this imagery,
or Divine Imagination…The way scientifically to work out a
problem is daily in thought to conceive of it as already being
an accomplished fact in experience.*

– Ernest Holmes

*Being against war is not at all the same thing as being for
peace. Holding a positive image, vividly imagining a state of
peace to exist, contributes to that state's coming about in ways
that may seem quite mysterious if we have too limited a belief
about the capabilities of the human mind. Because of the
interconnectedness of all minds, affirming a positive vision
may be about the most sophisticated action any one of us
can take.*

– Willis Harman

Creating Peace within Yourself

37

Go on a vision quest of peace

Native Americans marked the transition of young boys into manhood through vision quests. An adolescent boy was sent into the desert or forest for several days or longer, dependent only on himself for survival, until he received a vision of what his future would hold or what direction his life was to take. Today, numerous spiritual and adventure-oriented tour companies sponsor vision quests, with guided activities leading up to and following participants' solo journeys into the wilderness.

If this idea calls to you, check out what is available in your area and on-line. Then sign up for a guided quest to clarify your vision of peace. Or consider going on an extended solo camping trip, or taking short trips in nature, to contemplate what peace is for you. Chances are that your foray into the territories of self-reliance and silence will offer up new insights and inspiration for creating peace in your life.

38

Seek counsel for prolonged feelings that interfere with your inner peace

Sometimes, no matter what we do, we seem unable to shake our fears, anger, or grief. At these times, it is wise to reach out to someone who can give us a helping hand.

Seek out a counselor, psychologist, spiritual leader, healer, or other person you trust who can listen to you. If you are looking for advice, find a qualified professional. If you are seeking someone to just listen lovingly, choose a close friend or family member who can remain truly objective and who knows how to help you transform your feelings into faith, forgiveness, and joy.

59

39

Develop your intuition

Intuition differs from intellect in that it provides us with knowledge that seems to transcend available facts. Often appearing spontaneously, intuitive knowing gives us heart-inspired insights and understanding that are unreachable through reasoning and analysis. Intuition is, perhaps, evidence of our connection to what twentieth century psychiatrist Carl Jung referred to as the collective unconscious, a universal aspect of the psyche to which all individuals have access. As such, it offers us the promise of an expanded awareness that can create peaceful solutions to problems unsolvable by the intellect alone.

You can develop your intuition by paying attention to those moments when you are suddenly aware of a new insight that solves a long-standing problem or an *Aha!* that helps you understand a confusing situation. The more you acknowledge the messages you receive in this manner, the stronger your intuition becomes. Learning to access and accept intuitive information can ease your mind and contribute to your overall sense of well-being and peacefulness.

40

Live in the present

Sorrow and anger over past events, as well as fears and hopes for the future, are the greatest stumbling blocks to our ability to be at peace in the present. Yet, while it sounds like a simple task, remaining in the present entails more than just existing in the current moment.

Living in the present involves keeping our thoughts, emotions, and conversations focused on *now*. It means refusing to allow old memories and hurts or future hopes and plans, and the feelings they engender, to reside for any length of time in our minds or bodies.

When you notice that you are ruminating on what has already occurred or contemplating what might happen, gently bring your full attention back to the present. Open yourself up to the ever-unfolding possibilities offered by each moment.

Do it now…and now…and now.

61

The moment your attention turns to the Now, you feel a presence, a stillness, a peace. You no longer depend on the future for fulfillment and satisfaction—you don't look to it for salvation. Therefore, you are not attached to the results. Neither failure nor success has the power to change your inner state of Being. You have found the life underneath your life situation.

– Eckhart Tolle

Yesterday is history. Tomorrow is a mystery. And today? Today is a gift. That's why we call it the present.

– Babatunde Olatunji

41

Participate in a peace event

Joining others in the name of peace can augment our inner calm and contentment. It can also connect us with people of like mind and heart.

With a little research, it is relatively easy to find peace-related events or meetings where people with similar interests come together. For example, the Prayer Vigil for the Earth, which takes place every September in Washington, D.C., emphasizes individual and group prayers and features Native American elders. And the peace events and ceremonies sponsored throughout the year by the World Peace Prayer Society offer numerous opportunities for participation at varied locations around the country.

Be on the lookout for peace events in your area and make it a point to attend. Get on the mailing and e-mail lists of organizations whose mission you believe in to receive updates on their activities.

42

Be generous

Generosity is born of love. Its gift to the giver is as great as it is to the one who receives. As we open our hearts to others, we increase our capacity for inner peace and our desire to bring about peace in the world.

There are many ways to be generous with your time and attention, as well as with your money. Hand-made gifts, in-kind contributions to charities, volunteer service, and kindness to strangers are all loving and generous acts.

Find ways to share yourself with others and make it a point to do so on a regular basis. And remember to be generous with yourself as well by giving yourself the time and resources necessary to create and sustain your inner peace.

65

43

Balance work with play and renewal

The imbalance of work over play and renewal can lead to feelings of anxiety or depression, even illness. It can also cause us to lose our appreciation and zest for life. On the other hand, maintaining a balance between work, play, and renewal can enhance our capacity to cultivate and sustain inner peace.

66

Make time each day to relax and have fun. Take part in activities that bring you joy, either on your own or with people who energize you.

Giving yourself the opportunity to rest and renew your inner resources will increase your energy and your enjoyment of life. It may also improve your effectiveness at work.

44

Pay attention to your language

Words reveal our expectations, assumptions, and beliefs. They mirror our experiences of life and carry our intentions into the world to help create our experience of reality.

Pay attention to your internal dialogue and your spoken words to determine any thoughts that are inconsistent with your vision of peace. Use the table below for guidance.

The Words . . .	Tend to Communicate . . .
What if, must, have to	Fear or anxiety
Us/them, you/they	Anger or blame; exclusiveness
Not, can't, won't, don't, isn't...	What is NOT desired
We	Inclusiveness
Can, have, choose, enjoy, love	What IS desired
I am (sad/happy, afraid/confident, angry/loving, bad/good)	Whatever follows "I am" as true for the speaker

Explore the thoughts and beliefs that you uncover through your language to determine what serves you at this time in your life. Modify your thinking and speaking to bring any outdated thoughts and beliefs into alignment with your current vision of peace.

Also, pay attention to how you feel as you speak, to yourself and others, and practice using language that instills peaceful feelings within you.

We are what we think. All that we are arises with our
thought. With our thoughts we make the world…
Speak or act with a pure mind and happiness will
follow you as your shadow, unshakable.

– The Dhammapada

Train your mind in strong, impartial, and gentle thought;
train your heart in purity and compassion; train your tongue
to silence and to true and stainless speech…So living, without
seeking to convert, you will convince; without arguing, you
will teach; not cherishing ambition, the wise will find you out;
and without striving to gain men's opinions, you will subdue
their hearts.

– James Allen

Every time you have a thought, the biochemical/electro-
magnetic resistance along the pathway carrying that thought
is reduced. It is like trying to clear a path through a forest.
The first time is a struggle because you have to fight your way
through the undergrowth. The second time you travel that way
will be easier because of the clearing you did on your first
journey. The more times you travel that path, the less resistance
there will be, until, after many repetitions, you have a wide,
smooth track which requires little or no clearing.

– Tony Buzan

45

Repeat…repeat…repeat

Each time we think, speak, and act in a particular way, we broaden and deepen the pathways in our brains related to those thoughts, words, and behaviors. This makes it easier to say or do the same thing again. In fact, we can generally form a new habit by repeating the same activity for twenty-eight consecutive days.

Use repetition to develop new habits of peace. Be patient and persistent. Remember that you are replacing old well-worn pathways with new ones.

46

Simplify your life

Many of us have so much to do that we often end up overbooked, over-extended, and overwhelmed. Simplifying our lives can help bring us peace of mind, as well as more time to nurture that peacefulness.

When was the last time you had a day to yourself?

Ask yourself the following questions:

- What are the priorities in my life?

- What do I already do that contributes to my inner peace and sense of fulfillment?

- What aspects of my life are energizing?

- What can I do to simplify my life?

Consider making a list of everything on your schedule for a week. Rank each item from five to one according to how much it helps you feel at peace (5 = It adds a lot; 4 = It adds some; 3 = It neither adds nor detracts; 2 = It detracts some; 1 = It detracts a lot).

Strive to reduce the number of activities with low scores, while increasing the number of activities with high scores, that you allow in your life.

47

Make conscious choices about what you read, listen to, and watch

Each of us is influenced, either consciously or unconsciously, by what we allow into our minds and hearts. Words and images of violence, despair, and other forms of negativity can disrupt our sense of peace, joy, and contentment.

Be mindful about the books, news articles, and magazines you read, the conversations and music that you listen to, and the television programs and movies you watch. The more positive the messages you see and hear, the more hopeful and peaceful you are likely to feel.

72

48

Practice radical forgiveness

Forgiveness is often more easily spoken about than granted. Yet it is one of the most promising tools for peace, primarily because of the change in consciousness that accompanies it. Forgiveness frees the forgiver from the confines and consequences of negative emotions and opens the heart to possibilities previously unknown.

Today's world cries out for the radical forgiveness of individuals seemingly beyond such blessing, offering us both the challenge and the opportunity to turn our lives around.

Make a list of people for whom you believe forgiveness is not an option. Then study spiritual and religious texts on the subject of forgiveness, most of which value and promote the act of forgiving.

Be the one who forgives.

73

Forgiveness releases us from the power of fear. It allows us to see with kindly eyes and rest in a wise heart…Forgiveness means giving up all hope of a better past.

– Jack Kornfield

Forgiveness does not mean we suppress our anger; forgiveness means that we have asked for a miracle: the ability to see through the mistakes that someone has made to the truth that lies in all of our hearts…There is no peace without forgiveness…If you can state, despite your resistance, your willingness to see the spiritual innocence, the light in the soul of one who has harmed you, you have begun the journey to a deep and unshakable peace.

– Marianne Williamson

Creating Peace within Yourself

49

Cultivate the qualities of admired peacemakers

Some people, both from the past and in the present, provide excellent role models for those of us searching for ways to promote peace. Each of these peacemakers had or has qualities that set them apart from their contemporaries.

Make a list of people whose peacemaking abilities you admire. Read about their private and public lives to determine the personal characteristics that you most admire in them.

Develop and refine these qualities within yourself.

50

Keep a journal of gratitude or peace

Gratitude is a steppingstone to inner peace. It is nearly impossible to feel upset and grateful or peaceful at the same time.

Count your blessings by keeping a gratitude journal, as recommended by Sarah Ban Breathnach in *Simple Abundance*. Write down, either daily or weekly, everything for which you feel thankful. Record both the little and big things in your life and keep the journal up to date.

You may also choose to keep a peace journal. Write down the times you have felt at peace during the day or week.

Begin to increase the amount of time you invest in the activities, people, and environments that you associate with gratitude and peace.

77

51

Surrender your worries to God

However good we get at handling our fear, anger, and despair, there are times when these problems are too big for us to endure and beyond the help of a friend or counselor. In these moments, it is essential that we learn to turn over our worries to a power greater than ourselves, by whatever name we know it.

When you find yourself in the midst of a crisis or overwhelmed by troublesome thoughts and feelings, ask for help from God, Allah, Christ, Buddha, or whomever you have come to call on in such times.

Once you have asked for divine intervention, let go of your worries and trust that your request is being granted.

78

52

Be committed to your inner peace regardless of what is going on around you

As we develop our sense of peace, it is important to learn how to maintain that inner peacefulness regardless of what we are doing or what is happening around us. Remember, whatever our external senses are telling us, it is possible to access the peace within.

Consider that your inner reality is yours to create. Your response to nonpeaceful situations and people is up to you.

It is easy in the world to live after the world's opinion;

it is easy in solitude to live after our own;

but the great man is he who in the midst of the crowd keeps

with perfect sweetness the independence of solitude…

Of your own accord you cling to your unrest; of your own

accord you can come to abiding peace…

You can obtain freedom and peace alone by your

own efforts, by yielding up that which binds the soul,

and which is destructive of peace.

– James Allen

Creating Peace with Your Family and Friends

The peace you give is equal to the peace you live.

Peace begets peace. The more peaceful we become, the greater peace we offer the people around us, especially those who are close to us on a regular basis. As such, we become both champions and role models for peace.

Peace with family and friends centers on maintaining an awareness of our common humanity and our loving connections. It thrives on our ability to keep our hearts open and to consistently act from love in these important relationships.

As you begin to focus on helping create peace with and among your family and friends, remember to empower them with responsibility for their own peace and to accept that they are following their own paths and timing. Avoid judgmental thoughts or actions that might usurp the choices of the people you love. And refrain from comparing your ability to nurture and sustain inner peace with the peacefulness of others.

There are plenty of opportunities to co-create peace with your loved ones. In this section are ways you can work with family members and friends to engender peace both among and beyond your immediate circle of influence. Select those activities for which you have an affinity and feel free to adopt suggestions from the other two sections of the book for use with those you love.

53

Involve your children in creating peace

As Art Linkletter and Bill Cosby have proven, kids say the darnedest things. Speaking honestly and from the heart, kids often express profound insights about life.

Ask your children (or the children of friends and family members) the following questions:

- What does peace mean?

- What does peace feel like?

- What does peace look like?

- When are you most peaceful?

- How do you know when you have peace?

- What is the most important thing you can do to create peace?

- What do you think *I* can do to be more at peace?

54

Convene a family meeting about creating and sustaining peace in your family

The wisdom of a group of people is frequently greater than that of any one person in the group, especially when participants are of different genders and ages. Hence, involving your entire family in how to keep the peace among family members can increase the probability that such a peace can be achieved.

Hold a meeting with all adults and children in your immediate family to define your common goals for family peace. Give everyone a chance to be heard as you come up with ideas on how to accomplish these goals.

Keep the meeting positive, productive, and focused on solutions.

Schedule periodic meetings to assess how well everyone is doing and make adjustments as required.

83

55

Start a family scrapbook of articles and stories about peace, love, and beauty

Although the news and entertainment media tend to report on conflict, violence, and scandal, it is possible to find newspaper and magazine articles that speak to the heart and stir the soul. By paying attention to life-affirming stories, we can strengthen the peace, love, and beauty in our lives.

Make the collection of positive stories a family affair. Ask each person to watch and listen for stories that affirm his or her vision of peace, including associated qualities such as love, beauty, respect, kindness, generosity, and compassion. Consider articles and images from various media, as well as hand-written or typed stories from family members that describe their positive personal experiences and observations.

Gather everyone together periodically, perhaps once a month, to see and talk about what each family member has found. Then put all the items in your scrapbook.

84

56

Pray for or meditate on peace with friends and family members

The power of prayer and meditation is magnified exponentially when two or more people gather together for these purposes. In addition, meditating with others is often easier than meditating alone.

Add a prayer for peace to the blessings offered at meal or bed times. Remember that once you have asked for peace, giving thanks for peace is a good way to acknowledge your trust that your prayer has been answered.

Set up specific times to pray for or meditate on peace with your friends, family, or both. Invite people to bring their favorite peace prayers and meditations to share. When meditating, you may choose to direct peace and loving kindness to specific locations throughout your community and the world, or to just allow the peace that naturally comes from meditation to permeate the group and radiate outward.

85

Ask, and it will be given you;
seek, and you will find;
knock, and it will be opened to you.
For everyone who asks receives,
and he who seeks finds,
and to him who knocks, it will be opened.

– Matthew 7:7-8

Having established a radiant center in your being, you can let
loving kindness radiate outwardly and direct it wherever you
like…This extension (of your emotional being) matures as you
purposefully direct loving kindness toward people you have a
hard time with, toward those you dislike or are repulsed by,
toward those who threaten you or have hurt you.

– Jon Kabat-Zinn

Creating Peace with Your Family and Friends

57

Bring in the new year with loved ones by envisioning peace

The beginning of a new year is a superb time to clarify and proclaim our intentions for the next twelve months. Joining with friends and family members to create a collective vision of peace for the upcoming year adds a valuable dimension to New Year's Day celebrations. In addition, the group's shared focus helps strengthen and energize the vision.

Invite your loved ones to welcome the new year with you, either on New Year's Eve or during the first few days of the new year. Give each person time to think about and write down his or her vision of peace.

Ask people to write in the present tense, using statements such as "We are . . . ," "It is . . . ," and "I am . . ."

Have each person read what she or he has written. Or place all statements in a container and allow each person to select and read someone else's vision.

You may choose to collect and assemble all the statements into a single vision for peace to share with others.

58

Resolve a conflict with someone you love

It can be easy to allow a misunderstanding or disagreement to create a rift with someone we love. It can also be tempting to allow that estrangement to continue, by either fanning the flames of anger and mistrust or by burying the associated pain. Yet holding on to or hiding from conflicts, especially with loved ones, restricts our access to inner peace, and curtails the peace we have with family and friends.

Identify someone currently in your life with whom you have an unresolved conflict. Focus on your heart's desire for your relationship with this person until you are aligned with healing the problem between you. When you are ready, speak lovingly and openly to him or her about your choice to mend the relationship and work together to find a win-win outcome.

Be willing to accept your contribution to the issue and to forgive the actions of your loved one, as well as yourself.

If talking with the person is impossible, or likely to escalate the conflict, use prayer and meditation to resolve the problem within yourself.

Consider repeating this process until you have restored the loving relationships with all the loved ones currently in your life.

59

Refrain from participating in others' arguments

Arguments are full of powerful energy. They can carry anger, resentment, fear, jealousy, greed, hatred, and other limiting emotions that feed on the energy of anyone in their vicinity.

Learn to remain centered in peace when you are in close proximity to the arguing of others, especially when the conflict is among relatives and friends. Refuse to participate or be drawn into the argument. Remove yourself from the situation if necessary.

Once you are able to maintain your own peace while others argue, you may choose to add peaceful energy to a volatile situation, and perhaps help diffuse an argument, through peaceful interaction. Do this *only* if you can remain loving toward all parties, in both your thoughts and your words, and detached from the content of the argument.

60

Be aware of what you are thinking, saying, and listening to concerning the people close to you

Quantum physics asserts that there is no such thing as objective obser-vation at the subatomic level. The very act of observation influences the appearance of that which is being observed. In a similar fashion, when we put our attention on the specific qualities or behaviors of the people around us, we can influence what we see. Our thoughts and words can have an effect on all the people involved.

Pay attention to the thoughts that you allow to occupy your mind, especially when it comes to your beliefs and expectations regarding the people you love. You do them a disservice by thinking badly of them or holding on to unrealistic expectations. On the other hand, you help them immeasurably by focusing on their good qualities and accepting them for who they are.

Be aware of what you say about the people you love. Talk about your friends and family members only in ways that respect and empower them. In addition, refrain from participating in gossip or listening to derogatory remarks about the people in your life.

91

What we perceive depends upon what we look for.

– Gary Zukov

Your mind is a creative medium; therefore, what you think and feel about the other, you are bringing to pass in your own experience…You are the only thinker in your world. You are responsible for the way you think about the other.

– Joseph Murphy

61

Teach peace by example

People respond as much or more to what we do than to what we say. This is especially true with children, for whom our actions tend to speak louder than our words.

Demonstrate peacefulness in your interactions with others. Whether you are talking with friends about controversial issues or disciplining your children, remain calm and at peace as you speak. Use effective conflict resolution techniques to diffuse arguments in your family and to keep peace with friends.

Make your day-to-day actions consistent with the consciousness of peace.

62

Make peace with past lovers, spouses, friends, and alienated family members

Past hurts can accumulate in the body and clutter the mind, making it difficult to move forward in life. Finding ways to make peace with former lovers, spouses, and friends, as well as alienated family members, frees us to grow in love. It also releases others from being tied to us through our negative thoughts or beliefs.

Make a list of people no longer in your life whom you feel have hurt you. Then forgive and release each person, one by one, through meditation, imagination, prayer, or another method that works for you. Continue until you have made peace with everyone on your list.

Here is one technique that can be especially helpful in letting go of old hurts: Sit quietly for a few minutes and clear your mind. Take two or three deep breaths. When you feel calm, begin to focus on your heart while remembering a person, pet, or circumstance that engenders unconditional love within you. Stay centered in this feeling of love for several minutes. Then, while remaining in the feeling of love, bring an image of a person from your list into your heart. Hold both the image and the feeling of love in your heart as long as you can. Repeat this process until you can easily associate the image with love.

63

Share your knowledge and ideas about peace with your family and friends

It is fun to share our passion for peace with others. We may ignite a spark of interest in another person that burns brightly for a long time. Plus, we may discover others who are eager to work with us on peace projects that are near and dear to our hearts.

Talk about peace with your family and friends. Tell them what peace means to you and what you are doing to remain peaceful in your life and to help create peace in the world. Invite them to share their thoughts and experiences of peace with you, and listen openly to their ideas.

Remember to respect other points of view and remain peaceful during your conversations.

64

Listen attentively with an open mind and heart

Listening is an art. To truly listen to someone is to remain empty of our own opinions and willing to learn something new. This ability to listen to another, without having or promoting our own agendas, helps us feel peaceful within ourselves. It also generates goodwill and strengthens our relationships with those we love.

Practice listening with an open mind and heart. Remain peaceful and pay full attention to what your husband, wife, partner, or child is saying. Expect to gain new insights while listening to a friend. Be especially vigilant in listening attentively to someone with ideas that differ from yours.

...listening is more than just not interrupting.
It is acknowledging through one's active attention
that the other person is being heard. Perhaps most
important is that people who are sharing their feelings
be assured that they will not be criticized for having
such feelings.

– Riane Eisler

65

Empower your friends to make their own choices regarding peace

When we begin to focus on creating peace with our friends, we may discover that we enjoy being with some friends more than with others. Likewise, our peacefulness is likely to appeal more or less to various friends. This is natural.

Trust that your emphasis on inner and outer peace will strengthen the friendships that serve you. Be loving and honest with all your friends and empower them to make their own choices about creating and sustaining peace in their lives.

As your friends determine how they will live, you can support their choices from near or far, depending on how you feel in their presence. Remember to empower yourself, as well as your friends, by doing what enhances your choices regarding peace.

66

Avoid responding in anger

Words gain strength when accompanied by strong emotions. Words of anger, when spoken from the feeling of anger, carry intense energy that can rupture relationships in ways that are challenging to repair.

The next time you are tempted to vent your anger toward someone you care about, stop. Give yourself as much time as necessary, perhaps removing yourself from the situation, until you can express how you feel in a caring way. While you may still feel anger, allow yourself to reconnect with your heart before you speak.

67

Create a family montage of peace

A montage is an assortment of images and words that exemplifies a specific topic. It speaks to the head and the heart and imprints its message at both conscious and subconscious levels.

Engage your entire family in creating a montage of peace. Attach pictures and text from magazines, hand–made drawings, and other items to a large poster board to symbolize what peace means to your family.

Place the poster where everyone will see it often.

68

Recognize signs of separation and build unity

Our relationships with those we care most deeply about offer us repeated chances to act either from fear and anger or from faith and forgiveness. Fear, anger, and other so-called negative emotions arise most often when we feel separated from others, from our own inner peace, and from a source of power greater than ourselves. Faith and forgiveness come from feelings of *oneness* with others and an alignment with our true selves and the divine in all life.

Learn to recognize signs of separation in your intimate relationships: an ongoing desire to pull back or control, unexplained irritability, judgments about others, impatience, unfounded feelings of being hurt, and chronic low self-esteem. Acknowledge these aspects of your whole self, without judgment. Then do what you know aids you in reconnecting with your own inner peace, with the love of God, and with family and friends.

Only through our connectedness to others can we really know and enhance the self. And only through working on the self can we begin to enhance our connectedness to others.

– Harriet Goldhor Lerner

The bond of our common humanity is stronger than the divisiveness of our fears and prejudices. God gives us the capacity for choice. We can choose to alleviate suffering. We can choose to work together for peace. We can make these changes—and we must.

– Jimmy Carter

69

Teach your favorite songs of peace to children

Most children love to sing. Their tendency to repeat the songs they know reinforces the messages of those songs, for them and for you.

Organize a peace sing–a–long with your children and their friends. Or teach peace songs to your kids as you travel in the car. Consider helping a group of children put on a peace concert for your neighbors and friends.

Sing loud. Sing often.

70

Plant a family peace garden

Planting bulbs in the fall and seeds in the spring is a common event in many families. Watching the resulting flowers and vegetables appear, seemingly out of nowhere, is like witnessing a magician at work.

Start a tradition of imbuing the bulbs and seeds you plant with what peace means to you. Have each member of the family designate what qualities certain seeds represent, calling each one out as the seeds are planted. For example, you might plant seeds of love, harmony, having everyone on earth well fed, peace between specific countries, a cooperative Congress, and so on.

Then enjoy Mother Nature's magic show as you watch your seeds of peace grow!

71

Use your imagination to create peace in your personal relationships

When we are in the middle of a conflict with someone important in our lives, it can be challenging to see around the problem. Our imaginations, however, can leap over the problem and actually experience the solution.

The next time you find yourself in a conflict with a family member or friend, use your imagination to explore a positive outcome. Sit quietly and imagine that the problem has already been solved. Jump forward in your imagination and, without knowing how the change occurred, focus on what your relationship with this person is like now that the conflict has been resolved to each person's benefit.

Be present in the solution. Notice what you see, hear, and feel. Imagine what you are saying to this person and what he or she is saying to you. Allow yourself to bask in the positive experience for as long as you can.

Repeat this exercise often. Then carry your good feelings and images with you when you are with the other person.

Act as if your positive outcome is true.

72

Focus on the feeling of reaching your goals and imagined outcomes, especially those involving family and friends

Throughout our lives we are taught to set goals for ourselves. Although this is essentially a good practice, it can lead us to believe that our goals are the best and only possible outcomes. Additionally, because our goals often involve the people we most care about, we end up projecting our ideas of success onto them. When we become attached to a specific result or imagined outcome, for ourselves or for others, we may be closing the door on something even better.

Experiment with holding loosely and lightly the specific details of your goal or imagined outcome. After identifying your goal or experiencing your imagined outcome, focus *only* on the feelings associated with attaining what you desire. By embodying the feelings of success, you remain in charge of your actions related to your goal or outcome, while allowing for the possibility of an even greater result.

This process works especially well when your goal or imagined outcome involves other family members or friends. As you detach yourself from the specific details of success, you make room for the collective wisdom of all involved, as well as for the hand of God.

110

I am cognizant of the interrelatedness of all communities
and states . . . We are caught in an inescapable network of
mutuality, tied in a single garment of destiny.
Whatever affects one directly, affects all indirectly.

– Martin Luther King, Jr.

We are members of one human family, one human dignity,
one human worth.

– Imam Izak-El Mu'eed Pasha

When we are dreaming alone, it is only a dream.
When we are dreaming with others,
it is the beginning of reality.

– Dom Helder Camara

Creating Peace in Your Community, Nation, and the World

We are one.

The earth is a living organism on which all of life is interconnected. In a sense, the planet is like a single body with various parts, including the land, water, plants, insects, and animals. The continued existence of any one part depends, to varying degrees, on the activities and conditions of the other parts. No single part can be injured without affecting the rest of the body. Likewise, whatever enhances or heals one part contributes to the health of the whole.

Overlaid on the natural body of the earth are the invisible boundaries between nations, states, counties, municipalities, and neighbors. These divisions add geopolitical, economic, and cultural dimensions to our interdependence, with all the concomitant differences in language, customs, and religious beliefs. Yet the survival of each entity still depends on the activities and health of the people next door. And the world body remains viable only with the cooperation of all its parts.

The good news is that, because we are all interconnected, the positive actions of a small number of people can have tremendous impact on the lives of many more. Therefore, in addition to sustaining inner peace and joining with neighbors and friends, you can play an important role in creating peace in your community, nation, and the world.

In this section are a variety of ways you can help create peace on earth. Select the suggestions to which you are most drawn. Consider exploring a few that make you stretch. And remember to review the other two sections for activities you can adapt to your peace work with others.

Part Two: Deepening Peace is especially helpful for carrying out the ideas in this section.

111

73

Smile

A smile is a mood–altering event. It uplifts the person who sees it and brings a sense of well–being to the person on whose face it appears.

Be sure to smile when you are feeling happy. Experiment with smiling when you are feeling "blue." Smile at your boss and employees, the dry cleaner, store clerks and people waiting on tables, receptionists, the person in the toll booth, and total strangers.

Smile for no reason.

74

Build relationships with your neighbors

In this highly mobile and busy society, people frequently live somewhere for years without ever getting to know their neighbors. Yet the sense of belonging and community that comes from having good relationships with the people who live close by is ample reward for the effort. And the connections we make with neighbors can both contribute to and reflect our inner and outer peace.

Make it a point to meet and know your neighbors. Start by welcoming newcomers with a loaf of bread or a bouquet of flowers. Offer to water your neighbors' plants or collect their mail while they travel. Ride-share or take turns driving your children to school and sports events. Organize a block party, start a book club, or hold a community yard sale.

As you get to know the people in your building or on your street, talk about what is important in your respective lives. Build deep relationships with those neighbors to whom you feel closely connected. Who knows? Some of them may join you in your actions for peace.

113

75

Take peace to work

Most of us log in a considerable number of hours at work, day after day, week after week, and year after year. Our work is often demanding and stressful, posing a threat to our inner peace. The tensions from our work lives can even spill over into our nonworking hours, making it a challenge to sustain our peacefulness at home.

Doing work that is meaningful to you and with which you are fully aligned is a powerful way to experience peace at work. Even then, however, there are days when specific techniques can help you retain your inner peace.

Explore ways to sustain your peacefulness at work. Play soothing music, take time out for prayer or meditation, go for a walk during lunch, or read inspiring literature during your coffee or tea times. Practice maintaining your consciousness of peace during meetings and when emergencies erupt. Take time or use affirmations to regain your inner calm before responding to difficult requests or situations.

76

Be of service

Being of service is considered a virtue in the majority of faith traditions. Siddha Yoga, for example, encourages the attitude of selfless service (*seva*), which involves the ability to remain focused on a higher purpose and connected to the divine, while performing any and all tasks. The aim of *seva* is to serve God by serving others, with no expectation of personal acknowledgment or reward.

Practice being of service as you go about your daily activities. Volunteer to work for an organization or group whose goals are in line with your ideas of peace and its associated issues, such as poverty, hunger, literacy, human rights, and so forth. Whether you are serving God or helping others, your attitude of service can turn even the most menial tasks into loving actions and contribute to the well–being of those you serve.

115

The essence of sacred service dwells in the mind. When a person's thoughts are connected to Divine wisdom and nobility, even the simplest actions become holy.

– Baal Shem Tov

We serve others by extending our state of mind. If the energy which emanates from our presence is uplifting, we will uplift others. If our energy is clear and peaceful, those around us will experience a greater sense of clarity and peace.

– Susan S. Trout

The structural core of every religion is some form of prayer or communion with the Divine, combined with love and service to fellow beings. The essence of every religion is an experience of the heart.

– Sri Swami Satchidananda

Creating Peace in Your Community, Nation, and the World

77

Attend religious services different from your own

Much of the conflict in the world seems to focus on religious differences and an intolerance for seemingly contradictory points of view. Yet most religions eschew violence and promote love, compassion, and tolerance.

The late Reverend Sri Swami Satchidananda, a Yoga Master and spiritual teacher, advocated a universal view of faith. Stating that, "Truth is one, paths are many," he conducted interfaith services around the world to help bring together people of all backgrounds and beliefs.

Learn about the essential teachings of religions other than your own. Identify similarities. Select a faith that intrigues you and arrange to attend a service in your area.

Go with an open mind and heart.

Consider replicating some of the sacred rituals from faith traditions other than your own in your home or place of worship. Your experience of and reverence for all forms of worship can help build unity and peace, both within and around you.

78

Sign a petition for peace

Petitions have become a useful way of promoting a particular viewpoint. They are usually forwarded by their sponsors to people with policy-making and decision-making authority related to the issue at hand.

Search the Internet and check with peace organizations to find petitions for peace. Sign and pass along those that best express your ideas regarding peace.

79

Support organizations and projects that promote peace

There are many well-established and new organizations that promote peace, along with others that focus on addressing the problems frequently associated with war and unrest, including poverty and hunger, human rights violations, environmental degradation, and religious intolerance. Contributing your time or money to these organizations helps ensure their continued operation and success.

Learn about the various organizations that are taking actions you believe will help alleviate the conditions leading to violence, or that are making inroads toward creating and sustaining peace. Give generously to those groups whose missions and actions speak to your heart. Join and take an active role in an organization with goals that relate to your vision of peace.

Consider registering on-line with your selected groups to keep abreast of their activities and be alerted to opportunities for participating in their organized actions for peace.

80

Nurture and encourage the goodness in everyone

Each person exhibits a mixture of traits and habits that may be con-sidered as either pleasing or annoying. Ironically, the behaviors we choose to focus on in others can become even more pronounced, since we are likely to experience more of whatever we are paying attention to.

If you find yourself harshly judging another, stop, look, and listen for something good in that person. It may be a special quality, skill or ability, or expertise. Then make it a point to expose and expand that goodness through your interactions with the person.

If you are continually annoyed or frustrated by someone, take note of what it is that bothers you. Other people often act as mirrors, reflecting back to us what it is that we resist or reject in ourselves. When you have identified the specific quality or behavior that led to your reaction, take an honest look at yourself to see if you have hidden or avoided this "problem" in yourself. When you discover how you have related to this issue, you are likely to have more compassion for the other person.

Your understanding and compassion, and your willingness to shine a light on the goodness of others, serve to enhance their well-being and yours.

Goodness is the only investment that never fails.

– Henry David Thoreau

*Don't waste yourself in rejection, nor bark against the bad,
but chant the beauty of the good.*

– Ralph Waldo Emerson

*Life has a bright side and a dark side, for the world of relativity
is composed of light and shadows. If you permit your thoughts
to dwell on evil, you yourself will become ugly. Look only
for the good in everything (so) that you absorb the quality
of beauty.*

– Paramahansa Yogananda

Creating Peace in Your Community, Nation, and the World

81

Sponsor a child or community in another country

Many people see a direct relationship between the prospect of peace and the elimination of poverty, hunger, illiteracy, and disease, especially among the world's children. They believe that giving people hope and the chance to have healthy and productive lives is an essential way to invest in the future and improve the prospects for lasting peace.

If this idea appeals to you, investigate various charitable organizations that have programs through which you can sponsor a child, either in another country or in the United States. Your monthly donation can help feed, clothe, and educate a child who might otherwise suffer throughout his or her entire life.

Consider organizing your community or an organization to which you belong to sponsor a small village or community in another country. Explore available options for sending needed supplies, as well as encouraging letters, to your adopted community.

124

82

Support school programs related to conflict resolution, mediation, and peace

Many young people are open to learning and applying conflict resolution and mediation techniques, especially among their peers. Their inherent and acquired skills in effectively creating and sustaining peace may be our best hope for world peace in the future.

Find out about the conflict resolution, mediation, and peace-related programs in your local schools. Support those that have a proven track record, work to improve those that are falling short of their goals, and lobby for new programs where they are needed. Get your children involved in these programs and use the same methods to solve problems at home.

Consider lending your support to school speakers and trips emphasizing conflict resolution, teamwork, diversity, nonviolence, and human rights, as well as exchange student programs and curricula that include the study of other cultures and current events around the world.

83

Start or join a peace circle

Peace circles, like those organized and promoted by the Global Renaissance Alliance (listed in Part Two), are composed of a handful of people who meet regularly to articulate a shared vision of peace and to meditate or pray for peace. Their ongoing gatherings provide a powerful way to keep peace alive, both for participants and for people around the world.

126

Join or initiate a peace circle in your community. Or consider creating a peace circle in your family.

84

Be a witness for peace

When people are bombarded by stories of conflict, unrest, terrorism, and the possibility of war, they tend to feel discouraged, depressed, or angry. Stories of peace, win–win solutions, and effective peacemaking activities, on the other hand, can lead to feelings of hope and love.

Be a witness for peace by sharing stories of peace and successful peace-making efforts with others. Scour news articles and the Internet for inspiring tales. Then do one or more of the following:

- Create and distribute a monthly or bi-monthly newsletter of peace to your friends and family members via mail or e-mail

- Write an article or letter to the editor of your local newspaper, or call in to a radio talk show, to acknowledge successful peacemaking efforts

- Start a web site containing and calling for stories of peace and peacemaking

- Initiate a peace story collection drive at your place of worship or work.

Promote peace.

*When we see the Spirit of Peace in action we need to honor it,
so it will grow. To become part of our everyday culture, peacebuilding activities need to be known, seen, and heard about.
We need a promotion campaign for peace.*

– Louise Diamond

Creating Peace in Your Community, Nation, and the World

85

Get to know someone from a different culture

It seems to be human nature to be cautious, and sometimes distrusting, of people about whom we know very little. We often see only what makes us different.

Get to know someone whose religion, ethnic background, or country of origin differs from yours. Set aside any preconceived notions you may have and approach the person with a child's curiosity and openness. Ask questions. Listen attentively.

Search for and build upon what you have in common.

86

Help a group of children make a peace quilt

Children's visions of peace inspire us because they represent the promise of peace for future generations. They also prompt us to take actions now to ensure that such peace is possible.

In September 2000, the Masters Group in Washington, D.C., initiated "The Children's Cloth of Many Colors," modeled after a mile-long cloth made by thirty-three nations. The ongoing project involves having children create a three-by-three-foot quilt by imbuing patches of cloth with their visions of what peace means. The completed quilts, which might contain pieces from a child's favorite dress, a winning sports jersey, a beloved bear or doll, or a baby blanket, are displayed regularly at peace events and parades. Some are presented to individuals who have a recognized commitment to peace.

Check out sites on the Internet for this and other peace quilt projects. Then organize a group of children in your place of worship, community, neighborhood, or local school to create a peace quilt.

87

Display symbols of peace

One of the simplest ways to make a statement for peace is to display peace symbols on your car or around your home. Both the peace flag and the Earth Day flag transcend national boundaries and offer messages of hope for the whole planet, as does the dove of peace. There are also many bumper stickers containing slogans for peace.

132

Find and display symbols of peace that communicate what is in your heart.

To take this a step further, consider demonstrating your community's commitment to peace by organizing a peace pole ceremony in a public location, such as a town square or a place of worship. More than 200,000 peace poles in more than 180 countries are currently displaying the message, "May peace prevail on earth," in multiple languages. The poles are available through the World Peace Prayer Society (listed in Part Two).

88

Love

Love is the cornerstone of peace. It is a key teaching in all religious and spiritual traditions. To truly love is to open ourselves to the grace of God.

Make important choices and take actions toward others *only* when you feel love, peace, and compassion toward yourself and everyone involved. When in doubt, wait until you have reframed how you view the situation or have transformed negative feelings into loving ones.

If you experience difficulty in feeling love for a particular person, focus on what you *can* love. Shifting your attention to love makes it possible for that love to grow until it embraces the person that you initially found hard to love.

Choose love.

133

*Neither violence, which destroys everything, nor intolerance,
which denies a person's identity, can build anything serious or
lasting: only solidarity can, guided and sustained by the force
of love, which generates, promotes, and renews everything.*

– Pope John Paul II

Every act of love is a work of peace, no matter how small.

– Mother Teresa

*Compassion and love are not mere luxuries. As the source
both of inner and external peace, they are fundamental
to the continued survival of our species.*

– The Dalai Lama

Creating Peace in Your Community, Nation, and the World

89

Study a country or culture about which you know little

Learning about people from different countries and cultures can expand our view of the world and help us be more tolerant and accepting of others. Such understanding can become a steppingstone to peace.

Identify a country or culture whose people you have distrusted or not fully understood. Take a course on your chosen topic or study it on your own as if you were taking such a class. Learn about the history, customs, beliefs, cultural heritage, values, and motivations of the people you have selected.

Remember to approach your study with an open mind, one that Zen Buddhists refer to as a "beginner's mind." Empty out any preconceived opinions you may have and start fresh.

Write a paper about the country or culture you have studied. Focus on the qualities you admire and the things you have in common.

Use your knowledge in your actions for peace.

90

Write a public letter about your vision of peace

Words, and the images they create, have power. The more frequently a particular point of view is stated, the stronger it becomes.

Write one or more letters to the editor of an area newspaper describing your vision of peace and addressing related topics such as compassion, forgiveness, respect, reverence for life, and love, as they relate to peace in your community, the nation, and the world. Encourage your friends and family members to do the same. Write from your heart.

Consider organizing a letter–writing campaign to strengthen the image and experience of peace in your community.

137

91

Visit terminally ill patients, especially children

Bearing witness to the suffering of others, especially young children, can be a poignant and profound experience. It can help us set aside our daily concerns and fully experience the preciousness of life. Such reverence for life is essential for lasting peace.

Volunteer to visit people in hospitals, nursing homes, hospices, and other care facilities. Your presence will have a positive effect on those you visit, while giving you a renewed appreciation for life.

This is truly a gift of love.

92

Live as if your choices and actions matter

If we see ourselves as separate from others, we may be more able to justify shortsighted, selfish, or destructive actions against them. Likewise, if we fail to understand how connected we are with all life, we may believe that our behavior affects only us or possibly those closest to us.

A separatist view of life is becoming increasingly difficult to rationalize as we witness the globalization of financial markets, worldwide climate changes, the spread of life-threatening diseases, and other signs of our interdependence. More and more we see that the choices and actions of a few people can have dramatic impact on the lives of many. Indeed, both fear and love can reverberate around the world.

Live each day as if your choices and actions have an effect on your family and friends, your neighbors, your nation, and people around the world. Because they do.

Remember, there is only one of us here.

139

Walk gently through life, for all the footfalls must
resound Respect.
Talk softly in life, for all the words must speak Kindness.
Act prudently in life, for all the deeds must manifest Peace.
Think compassionately in life, for all the thoughts must
echo Love.
In this Way do we live in a Sacred Manner.
In this Way do we reflect the soul of the Great Mystery.

– Mary Summer Rain

In a universe in which all things are infinitely interconnected,
all consciousnesses are also interconnected. Despite appearances,
we are beings without borders. Or as (David) Bohm puts it,
'Deep down the consciousness of mankind is one.'

– Michael Talbot

93

Have a "peace-in" at work or in your community or neighborhood

In the 1960s, many college students held sit-ins to make their views known to school administrators. They took a stand for a specific issue, or set of issues, by remaining in one place for a prolonged period of time, counting on their solidarity to call public and media attention to the topic at hand. This approach, when nonviolent, continues to have merit today.

Meet with the people in your neighborhood or from a local school to discuss having a "peace-in" for a day, a week, or longer. During that time, consider demonstrating your commitment to peace in one or more of the following ways:

- Display peace symbols
- Schedule a walk for peace
- Conduct a peace pole ceremony
- Put up posters and distribute flyers
- Hold a candlelight peace prayer vigil
- Insert quotations about peace in business literature
- Print a message of peace in the local newspaper
- Study peacemakers and peacemaking in school
- Contribute bake sale or car wash profits to a peace organization.

Be creative. Have fun. Advertise peace.

94

Take your vacation in another country

Visiting another country offers us a multitude of ways to help create peace in the world. We can enhance our personal understanding of another culture and share what we learn with our family and friends. We can also be ambassadors for peace while we visit.

Plan to take your next vacation in another country. Pay close attention to world conditions and pick a location where you are likely to feel and be safe. While you are there, make it a point to get to know as many residents as you can, develop a close relationship with a few residents, or stay with a local family. Exchange visions of peace and listen openly to inhabitants' opinions and experiences.

Consider combining your vacation with the gift of service. Check into options, such as those offered by the Sierra Club and Habitat for Humanity (listed in Part Two), for taking part in a project related to social, environmental, and other peace-related issues.

143

95

Learn and apply effective methods of conflict resolution and peacemaking

The more we know about proven methods for creating peace, the better equipped we are to remain at peace with the people in our lives. In addition, we may be able to use our knowledge to facilitate others in finding peace and to understand what might be effective in creating and sustaining peace at work and in the world at large.

Take courses in various methods of conflict resolution, mediation, and peacemaking. Read about successful efforts to create peace. Share what you learn with local and regional community groups and schools, as well as with people at work.

96

Use self-knowledge to foster peace

Self-knowledge is an important element in sustaining peace, both within ourselves and in our relationships with others. The more we are aware of our whole selves, including both the shadow and the soul, the more able we are to make conscious choices about interacting with others that are consistent with our visions of peace.

Make it a habit to identify your motives for acting in certain ways in your life. Look for patterns and seek to understand your underlying thoughts and feelings. Accept and love both the negative and the positive that exist within you. And learn to listen and respond to the deepest, truest aspect of yourself.

You may choose to seek professional counseling to more fully know yourself.

Use your knowledge of your true self to deepen your relationships with others in your community and to further your work for peace.

145

*It is possible to make significant, transformative changes
in the way we live each day in the human community.
We can find stable happiness; we can learn to have loving
and pleasurable relationships; we can be at peace…
If we aspire to discover the true self, to know what we
love and what we want, to be honest, and to take full
responsibility for our strengths and our weaknesses,
then we will be on our way.*

– Elizabeth Lesser

97

Be an audience for uplifting news stories, television programs, movies, magazines, and books

We live in a profit-driven economy. As consumers of the goods and services that produce sought-after profits, we have considerable power to influence what those products are. This is especially true when it comes to various forms of entertainment. With a concerted effort on the part of sufficient numbers of us, it could also be true for the news.

Be mindful of the news and television programs you watch, the movies you see, and the magazines and books you buy. Before becoming an audience for any of these things, ask yourself the following question:

- Are the images and words in this (news or television program, movie, publication) likely to enhance or detract from my sense of peace?

Act accordingly. Be an audience for peace.

98

Contact your representatives about your ideas for peace

The constitution of the United States, written in 1787, opens with the phrase, "We the people of the United States…" Today, we are those people, and it is both our right and responsibility to make our thoughts and wishes known to those whom we have elected to act on our behalf.

Let your local, state, and federal representatives know what you think and how you feel about peace. Write letters, make calls, and send e-mails concerning your point of view and your expectations for their actions.

Ask your representatives to address the difficult questions associated with attaining peace, such as the following:

- In what ways is military action a viable option for creating and sustaining peace?

- What are the underlying causes of terrorism and what can we do to eradicate them?

- How can we help people who have known *only* conflict and war to envision and embrace peace?

99

Host an exchange student in your home

Having someone from another country live with us provides us with an exceptional opportunity to learn about that person and her or his homeland. The experience also gives us the chance to promote peace and understanding on a personal level.

Inquire about exchange student programs in your area. Read available literature and talk to others who have hosted a foreign student in their homes to clarify what you might expect and what is expected of you.

When you are ready, open your door and your heart to an exchange student.

100

Join with others to pray for or meditate on peace in the world

The inner peace of a single individual can often be felt by the people nearby. Similarly, the peaceful energy generated by a group of people meditating together can have an effect on the surrounding population. For example, when a large group of meditators met a number of years ago in Washington, D.C., the crime rate in the city went down nearly 20 percent while the practitioners were holding their meditation sessions.

When the consciousness of a small group of people helps alter the thoughts or behavior of a large number of people outside the group, the situation is often referred to as having reached a *critical mass*. This phenomenon raises the possibility that, if enough people attune themselves to peace at the same time, the energy of peace can radiate out from the group to envelope and enrich the lives of people outside the group.

Participate in group contemplative activities, such as the annual Slow Walk for Peace sponsored by the Shalem Institute for Spiritual Formation (listed in Part Two). Or organize group meditations or prayers for peace in your place of worship or with organizations working for peace.

When praying, give thanks for peace, love, harmony, and unity. When meditating, build up the group's energy of peace and send it out to those in need within your community and around the world.

151

As citizen-diplomats of the world, we send peace as conscious expression wherever, whenever, and to whomever it is needed…Active citizenship begins with an envisioning of the desired outcome and a conscious application of spiritual principles…

– Congressman Dennis J. Kucinich

101

Support changes in government that you believe will facilitate peace

Our democratic form of government gives us repeated opportunities to contribute to peace in our country and around the globe. They include electing officials we believe are committed to peace and supporting proposed governmental changes that make world peace more possible.

Follow your heart and take an active role in assuring that your government keeps peace on its agenda. Support local, state, and federal candidates whose views are aligned with yours, by contributing your time or money to their campaigns.

Vote in every election.

Consider lending your support to the establishment of a cabinet–level U.S. Department of Peace, such as the one introduced to the House of Representatives in July 2001 (HR 2459, listed in Part Two). The stated purpose of this Department of Peace is to make nonviolence an organizing principle in our society, to help create peace in homes, families, schools, neighborhoods, cities, and the nation, as well as worldwide.

102

Encourage children to become pen pals with their peers in other countries

The earlier children learn about people in other countries and cultures, the less likely they are to develop prejudices that contribute to the distrust and enmity that thwart peacemaking efforts. Helping today's children develop understanding, acceptance, and respect for other life-styles and viewpoints is essential for tomorrow's peace.

Encourage the children in your family, neighborhood, and local schools to correspond with their peers from around the world. To get started, check out the Peace Pals program for children ages five to fifteen, sponsored by the World Peace Prayer Society (listed in Part Two), or look for other legitimate programs on the Internet.

You may choose to read the letters and e-mails of younger children, to make sure the communication remains appropriate and positive.

155

103

Honor diversity and build unity

Each person's perception of life is formed by his or her ethnicity, race, and culture, as well as the sum of his or her beliefs, assumptions, and personal experiences. With so much potential variability, we are bound to be different from each other in many ways. At the same time, we inhabit similar physical bodies, feel similar emotions, entertain similar thoughts, and strive to reach similar goals.

Honoring diversity and building unity are essential companions on the path to peace. Diversity without unity can lead to divisiveness and dissension, while unity without diversity can overlook individual strengths.

When you are in a situation where diversity and unity are issues, begin to create peace by acknowledging each person's unique contributions to the group. Then focus on what participants share, especially as it relates to their desired outcomes. By jumping ahead in time to what group members choose to have in the future, you are more likely to find common ground on which to build.

If some members get caught up in disagreements, gently return the group's attention to the agreed-upon goals. Ask each person to reaffirm his or her commitment to these results.

Consider studying and applying a dialogue process to help you address issues of diversity and unity in your work for peace.

104

Become an advocate for nonviolence

Two of the most respected peacemakers in history, Mohandas K. Gandhi and Martin Luther King, Jr., were proponents of nonviolence. It was their view that permanent peace is attainable only through peaceful means.

If you agree that *the means are the end*, and that only peaceful methods lead to lasting peace, become an advocate for nonviolence. Join an organization that promotes nonviolence, share your views with others, and remain peaceful in all your efforts to create peace in your life, your family, your community, your nation, and the world.

Be the peace you wish to see.

…I do not believe in short-violent-cuts to success…However much I may sympathize with and admire worthy motives, I am an uncompromising opponent of violent methods even to serve the noblest of causes…Experience convinces me that permanent good can never be the outcome of untruth and violence…

…Nonviolence is the greatest force at the disposal of mankind. It is mightier than the mightiest weapon of destruction devised by the ingenuity of man…

– Mohandas K. Gandhi (excerpts)

Peace is not merely a distant goal that we seek, but a means by which we arrive at that goal.

– Martin Luther King, Jr.

Creating Peace in Your Community, Nation, and the World

105

Organize a peace project

Some things are easier to do with others. Plus, it can be fun to work for a common cause with people we care about.

Organize a meeting with friends, co-workers, neighbors, and others who share your passion for peace. Explain your desire to contribute in some way to peace in your community or regional area and solicit ideas for projects from everyone.

Be sure to follow up on whatever the group decides.

106

Seek to understand the underlying causes of unrest in the world

Sometimes the reasons for unrest are plainly evident. At other times there are contributing causes that are much less apparent. Our prospects for peace, both locally and globally, are directly proportional to our ability to understand and address these underlying problems.

Identify a situation involving unrest or violence that interests you, in your community, the nation, or the world. Then research the issue.

Start with a "beginner's mind" by setting aside any opinions you may already have about that situation. Listen to what people on all sides of the issue have to say. Look into the historical development of the conflict. Consider the viewpoints of experts on this situation and related topics. Use alternative as well as mainstream sources of information. Be aware of destructive patterns of belief and behavior over time, as well as possible strategies for peace.

Imagine yourself walking in the shoes of all involved parties. Form your own opinion, without placing blame on any one person or group, about the underlying causes of the situation you have studied.

Use your knowledge to work for peace.

161

107

Be a consumer and investor for peace

In this country, we have countless options for how we spend and invest our dollars. The sheer enormity of possibilities means that putting our money where our hearts are can be both simple and complex. While the actions themselves are simple, the research and choices required to determine which actions to take can involve considerable time and attention.

Be a consumer and investor for peace by buying the products and stocks *only* of the companies that adhere to business practices consistent with your ideas of peace. You may, for instance, choose to support only those businesses that have humane working conditions, are environmentally friendly, demonstrate ethical management, or that have no connection to weapons or health hazards.

Make a list of the business practices that you choose to support. Then research the companies from which you are thinking about buying products or stock. Subscribe to publications that provide independent assessments of business practices or that list socially responsible companies, such as the *Green Money Journal* (listed in Part Two).

108

Believe in world peace

The consciousness of an individual is composed of that person's beliefs, assumptions, and personal experiences in life. The collective consciousness on the planet is made up of the combined consciousness of its inhabitants. As science is beginning to demonstrate, the interaction between our individual and collective consciousnesses is automatic and instantaneous. In other words, we are both influenced by and contribute to the consciousness, and the subsequent conditions, of the world.

Fortunately, there is growing evidence that a small group of committed people, known as a *critical mass*, can affect the consciousness and behavior of multitudes. What would happen if enough of us were able to replace our belief in war and violence with an unwavering belief in peace? How many of us would it take to shift the primary worldview from its tendency toward violence to the probability of peace?

Practice believing in peace. Each time you find yourself thinking or speaking of violence or from anger, fear, or retribution, make a conscious choice to shift your thoughts and words. Think instead from peace. Speak from peace. Maintain a consciousness of peace.

You may be the *one* that tips the scale toward peace on earth.

I believe in all that has never yet been spoken.

I want to free what waits within me

so that what no one has dared to wish

for may for once spring clear

without my contriving.

If this is arrogant, God, forgive me,

but this is what I need to say.

May what I do flow from me like a river,

no forcing and no holding back,

the way it is with children.

Then in these swelling and ebbing currents,

these deepening tides moving out, returning,

I will sing you as no one ever has,

streaming through widening channels

into the open sea.

– Ranier Maria Rilke

Creating Peace in Your Community, Nation, and the World

109

Develop the courage to discover how *you* reflect and contribute to discord in the world

It can be easy to sit in judgment about the violent actions of others, especially when they seem so far removed from how we see ourselves. On the other hand, if we have the courage to consider our own connection, however small, to a given situation, we may find that we are harboring some of the same thoughts or feelings that led those others to act.

Understanding that each person, to varying degrees, both *reflects* and *contributes* to the state of the world may seem difficult to accept. If true, however, this reflexive interconnectivity provides us with the perfect means to help create peace on earth. In essence, we can help heal the world by healing ourselves.

Whenever you are tempted to condemn an act of violence or hatred, ask yourself these questions:

- In what way(s) have I hurt someone recently?

- How often do I fail to listen to someone I care about?

- What thoughts or words of anger, fear, hatred, or despair have I recently entertained or expressed?

- Is there any emotion within me that counteracts peace and am I willing to transform it into something constructive?

110

Imagine world peace

Untold millions of young people around the globe have no personal experience of peace. Having grown up in war-torn countries, these children and young adults have no conceptual framework upon which to build images of peace. It is essential, therefore, for those of us who can do so to generate and hold within our hearts the sights, sounds, and sensations of peace.

The imagination is a powerful vehicle for peace. It is especially effective in a group setting. The shared intention and focus of a group imagination session, like the one offered in Part Two and summarized below, raises the energy and magnifies the probability of peace.

In a small or large group, guide participants to imagine peace in a predetermined situation. First, focus on the identified conflict. Second, go forward in time and imagine that peace exists in the situation, making it real by imagining what you see, hear, smell, and feel. Third, go even further forward in time and notice how life is different now that peace has prevailed for years. Next, feel grateful for the peace you are experiencing. Finally, come back from your imagined outcome. Believe that what you have imagined is true and carry the feelings of peace with you, while allowing for the actual results to be even better than you imagined.

Consider organizing youth groups to imagine world peace.

111

Be an instrument of peace

You are the most potent and creative instrument of peace. Like ripples in a pond, your inner peace and your peaceful actions extend farther and farther outward until you have helped transform people and situations beyond your knowing, thus creating new ripples upon ripples of peace.

State your intention each morning to be an instrument of peace, whether you will be alone, with family and friends, at work, or with others in your community. Reaffirm your commitment to peace as often as necessary throughout the day and do what you know helps you sustain your inner peace.

Dwell within peace
For peace is who you are
Deep within
Where only you and God reside

– Rae Thompson

PART TWO
Deepening Peace

Lord, make me an instrument of Thy peace;

where there is hatred, let me sow love;

where there is injury, pardon;

where there is doubt, faith;

where there is despair, hope;

where there is darkness, light;

and where there is sadness, joy.

O divine Master, grant that I may not so much

seek to be consoled, as to console;

to be understood, as to understand;

to be loved, as to love.

For it is in giving that we receive;

it is in pardoning that we are pardoned;

it is in dying that we are born to eternal life.

– St. Francis of Assisi

Peace Prayers

This section contains prayers for peace from individuals and most major religions and spiritual traditions around the world. Find and use those that speak to your heart, or create your own.

I offer you peace.
I offer you love.
I offer you my friendship.
I see your beauty.
I hear your need.
I feel your feelings.
My wisdom flows from the Highest Source.
I salute that Source in you.
Let us work together for unity and love.

– Mohandas K. Gandhi

May all beings everywhere plagued
with sufferings of body and mind
quickly be freed from their illnesses.
May those frightened cease to be afraid,
and may those bound be free.
May the powerless find power,
and may people think of befriending one another.
May those who find themselves in trackless, fearful wilderness—
the children, the aged, the unprotected—
be guarded by beneficent celestials,
and may they swiftly attain Buddhahood.

– Buddhist prayer for peace

173

O God, you have let me pass the night in peace,
let me pass the day in peace.
Wherever I may go upon my way
which you made peaceable for me,
O God, lead my steps.
When I have spoken, keep lies away from me.
When I am hungry, keep me from murmuring.
When I am satisfied, keep me from pride.
Calling upon you, I pass the day,
O Lord, who has no Lord.

– Boran prayer from Kenya

Deep peace of the running wave to you.
Deep peace of the flowing air to you.
Deep peace of the quiet earth to you.
Deep peace of the shining stars to you.

– Celtic prayer for peace

Blessed are the poor in spirit: for theirs is the kingdom of heaven.
Blessed are they that mourn: for they shall be comforted.
Blessed are the meek: for they shall inherit the earth.
Blessed are they which do hunger and thirst after righteousness:
for they shall be filled.
Blessed are the merciful: for they shall obtain mercy.
Blessed are the pure in heart: for they shall see God.
Blessed are the peacemakers: for they shall be called the children of God.

– Matthew 5:3-9

Help me spread your fragrance wherever I go.
Flood my soul with your Spirit and life.
Penetrate and possess my whole being so utterly
that my life may only be a radiance of yours.
Shine through me and be so in me that every soul I
come in contact with may feel your presence in
my soul.
Let them look up,
and see no longer me,
but only Jesus!
Stay with me and then I will begin to shine as you
shine, so to shine as to be a light to others.
The light, O Jesus, will be all from you;
none of it will be mine.
It will be you, shining on others through me.
Let me thus praise you in the way you love
best, by shining on those around me.
Let me preach you without preaching, not by
words but by my example,
by the catching force,
the sympathetic influence of what I do,
the evident fullness of the love my heart bears
for you.
Amen.

– Mother Teresa

The light of God surrounds us;
The love of God enfolds us;
The power of God protects us;
The presence of God watches over us.
Wherever we are, God is!

– James Dillet Freeman

God, give us grace to accept with serenity the things that cannot be changed, courage to change the things which should be changed, and the wisdom to distinguish the one from the other.

– Reinhold Niebuhr

O Lord, the Light of lights,
You are the Indweller of the entire Universe.
You are the Light of Awareness.
You are the Light of our Consciousness.
You are the One who enlightens everything and everybody.
You are the One who makes the sun shine, who makes the moon
    shine, who makes the stars shine, who makes the fire burn.
Kindly lead us to that Light of Wisdom and remove the darkness of ignorance.
Enlighten our hearts.
Help us experience that Light within and without.
Help us see the same Light, the same Spirit dwelling everywhere
    in everything, as everything.
Help us to understand You and You alone through all these various forms
    and names, through all these different approaches and ways of worship.
Help us recognize the central unity.
Help us realize that we are Your image, Your children, no matter what
    the differences are.
Let us behold Your Spirit running through all.
Give us the strength and courage and capacity to experience that Peace
    and Joy within and share that experience with everyone.
Help us to get away from these selfish temptations with which we are
    creating all the differences, all the fights, and all the wars.
We have suffered enough due to our ignorance.
Please guide us to know our brothers and sisters and to know that we are
    all parts of Your family.
Enlighten our paths, O Light of lights, Lord of lords. Help us. Guide us.

– Sri Swami Satchidananda

May thy peace and serenity bless us and the light of thy countenance shine upon our pathway henceforth and forever.

In the silence may we feel the holy presence of God, our Creator.

We open our hearts to the incoming of the light of God, praying that we may feel the impress of God's love drawing us all together in one spirit—those who are in the physical body, and the hosts in the world unseen.

We pray that we may realize this at-one-ment of spirit, and that during this service thy love may rise within our hearts and go out to all mankind, to all creation.

O gracious Spirit, we thank thee in humility for the expanding consciousness of thy goodness, thy love, in our hearts; and we thank thee for the knowledge of thy love and thy power to permeate our lives and lift them to thy world of beauty.

– White Eagle

Dear God,
Please remove from my mind the tendency to judge.
Please remove from my mind the tendency to hate.
Please remove from my mind the tendency to blame.
Please reveal to me, Lord, a way to stand in my power,
through love instead of fear, and
through peace instead of violence.
May I hear not the voice for anger, but only the voice for love.
And teach me, dear Lord, how not to hate those who hate me.
Transform all darkness into light, dear God,
And use my mind as an instrument of Your harmlessness.
I surrender to You my thoughts of violence.
Take these thoughts, Lord, and wash them clean.
Thank You very much. Amen.

– Marianne Williamson

Oh Lord, lead us from the
unreal to the real;
from darkness to light;
from death to immortality.
May there be peace in celestial regions.
May there be peace on earth.
May the waters be appeasing.
May herbs be wholesome, and may trees and
plants bring peace to all.
May all beneficent beings
bring peace to us.
May thy wisdom spread peace all through the world.
May all things be a source of peace to us.
Om Shanti, Shanti, Shanti (Peace, Peace, Peace)

– Hindu prayer for peace

Let us be united;
Let us speak in harmony;
Let our minds apprehend alike;
Common be our prayer;
Common be our resolution;
Alike be our feelings;
United be our hearts;
And perfect be our unity.

– Rig Veda

May your days be many and your troubles few.
May all God's blessings descend upon you.
May peace be within you, may your heart be strong.
May you find what you're seeking wherever you roam.

– Irish blessing

RIPPLES OF PEACE

May the Blessings of God rest upon you.
May His Peace abide with you.
May His Presence illuminate your heart,
Now and forevermore.

— Hazrat Inayat Khan

Send Thy peace, O Lord, that we may think, act, and speak harmoniously.
Send Thy peace, O Lord, that amidst our worldly strife, we may enjoy Thy bliss.
Send Thy peace, O Lord, that we Thy children on earth may all unite in
one family.

— Islamic prayer for peace

Oh God,
You are Peace.
From You comes Peace,
To You returns Peace.
Revive us with a salutation of Peace,
and lead us to your abode of Peace.

— Islamic prayer for peace

Lead me from Death to Life,
from Falsehood to Truth.
Lead me from Despair to Hope,
from Fear to Trust.
Lead me from Hate to Love,
from War to Peace.
Let Peace fill our Heart,
our World, our Universe.

— Jain prayer for peace

May the Lord bless you and guard you.
May the Lord show you favor and be gracious to you.
May the Lord show you kindness and grant you peace.

– Jewish prayer for peace

May we see the day when war and bloodshed cease,
when a great peace will embrace the whole world.
    Then nation will not threaten nation,
    and mankind will not again know war.
For all who live on earth shall realize
we have not come into being to hate or destroy.
    We have come into being
    to praise, to labor and to love.
Compassionate God, bless the leaders of all nations
with the power of compassion.
    Fulfill the promise conveyed in Scripture:
I will bring peace to the land,
and you shall lie down and no one shall terrify you.
    I will rid the land of vicious beasts
    and it shall not be ravaged by war.
Let love and justice flow like a mighty stream.
    Let peace fill the earth as the waters fill the sea.
And let us say: Amen.

– Jewish prayer for peace

181

Let us know peace.
For as long as the moon shall rise,
For as long as the rivers shall flow,
For as long as the sun shall shine,
For as long as the grass shall grow,
Let us know peace.

– Cheyenne prayer for peace

O Great Spirit of our Ancestors, I raise my pipe to you;
To your messengers the four winds, and to Mother Earth who provides
for your children.
Give us the wisdom to teach our children to love, to respect, and to be
kind to each other, so that they may grow with peace in mind.
Let us learn to share all good things that you provide for us on this Earth.

— Native American prayer for peace

Adorable presence,
Thou who art within and without,
    above and below and all around,
Thou who are interpenetrating
    every cell of my being,
Thou are the eye of my eyes,
    the ear of my ears,
    the heart of my heart,
    the mind of my mind,
    the breath of my breath,
    the life of my life,
    the soul of my soul.
Bless us, dear God, to be aware of thy
    presence in the East and the West,
    in the North and the South.
May peace and good will abide among
    individuals, communities, and nations.
This is my earnest prayer.
May peace be unto all!

— Swami Omkar

182

Peace flows through my heart, and blows through me like a zephyr.
Peace fills me like a fragrance.
Peace runs through me like rays.
Peace stabs the heart of noise and worries.
Peace burns through my disquietude.
Peace, like a globe of fire, expands and fills my omnipresence.
Peace, like an ocean, rolls on in all space.
Peace like red blood, vitalizes the veins in my thoughts
Peace like a boundless aureole, encircles my body of infinity.
Peace–flames blow through the pores of my flesh, and through all space.
The perfume of peace flows over the gardens of blossoms.
The wine of peace runs perpetually through the wine press of all hearts.
Peace is the breath of stones, stars, and sages.
Peace is the ambrosial wine of Spirit flowing from the cask of silence,
Which I quaff with my countless mouths of atoms.

– Paramahansa Yogananda

Give us, o God, the vision which can see thy love in the world, in
spite of human failure. Give us the faith to trust the goodness in
spite of our ignorance and weakness. Give us the knowledge that
we may continue to pray with understanding hearts, and show us
what each one of us can do to set forth the coming of the day
of universal peace.
Amen.

– Frank Borman/Apollo 8

One cultivates silence not by forcing the ears not to hear, but by turning up the volume on the music of the world and the soul.

– Thomas Moore

Peace Meditations

This section offers several meditations on peace. You can use them for your personal practice or adapt them for group meditations.

Embracing Inner Peace

Find a quiet place to sit comfortably, with your back straight and your feet flat on the floor. Set your intention to let go of your thoughts and attachments and to embrace your inner peace, joy, and love.

Close your eyes, relax, and focus only on your breath.

Release any thoughts, sensations, or emotions that arise. Just let them float away. If they reappear, imagine them leaving again with your breath. Be aware of the silence between your breaths.

Imagine your entire being filling up with light from deep within you, from your divine essence. Imagine this light emanating from your heart or your forehead in all directions. Notice that all else has disappeared and only the light remains.

Feel your oneness with the divine, with others who are meditating or praying for peace, and with all people in the world. Absorb and send forth universal love, light, joy, and peace.

When you are ready, bring your attention back to the present. Open your eyes.

Breathing Peace

— Created by Rev. Wilma Donald, Community Center for Wholistic Healing

Get into a comfortable position and close your eyes. Take a slow deep breath and hold it. Exhale slowly and completely relax your physical body.

PAUSE

Take another slow deep breath and hold it. Exhale slowly and completely relax your mind.

PAUSE

Take another slow deep breath and hold it. Exhale slowly and completely relax your emotions.

PAUSE

Bring to mind a time in your life when you were completely relaxed and at peace. Allow the memory of that peaceful time to permeate your physical, mental, and emotional self.

PAUSE

Now allow the feeling of harmony and peace to flow throughout your entire being. Ask for divine guidance and protection, and silently repeat to yourself

- I think thoughts of peace.

- I speak words of peace.

- I perform acts of peace.

- I share my peace with all others for the highest good of all.

- I abide in peace.

To the count of five, return to your outer consciousness in peace. One...two...three...four...five.

Radiating Peace

— Created by Rev. Wilma Donald, Community Center for Wholistic Healing

PREPARATION

Find a quiet place where you will not be disturbed. Turn off telephones and fax machines, and decrease the possibility of other distractions. Consider lighting a candle, burning incense, placing fresh flowers in your meditation space, or playing soft music. Sit comfortably, with your spine straight and your body relaxed. If you like, invite the divine energy of God, Allah, Christ, or another spiritual being to flow throughout your being as you begin to meditate.

187

MEDITATION

Close your eyes. Breathe slowly and deeply. As you exhale completely, allow your physical body to relax.

PAUSE

Take another slow deep breath. As you exhale completely, allow your mind to relax.

PAUSE

Take one more slow deep breath. As you exhale completely, allow your emotions to relax.

PAUSE

Sense the feeling of fluid warmth, like liquid light, starting to flow throughout your entire body. Beginning at the top of your head, feel this fluid warmth as it flows effortlessly down,

- over the top of your head,

- over your brow,

- over your eyes, relaxing the muscles around your eyes,

- down across your cheeks, relaxing the muscles around your mouth and inside your mouth as you allow your teeth to separate slightly.

Breathe normally now as this wonderful feeling of liquid light flows over your jaws and deep into the muscles of your neck,

- relaxing your neck muscles,

- flowing deep into the muscles of your shoulders, relaxing all the large and small muscles of your shoulders.

Allow the energy to flow all the way down your arms,

- relaxing your arms,

- flowing into your hands and out your fingertips.

Now feel the warmth of this liquid light as it flows deep into the muscles of your chest,

- relaxing the organs in your chest,

- relaxing every tiny cell in the muscles of your abdominal area.

Allow the light energy to flow into and relax your lower body, your hips, your thighs, your knees, calves, and ankles. Feel the energy as it flows into your feet and out the tips of your toes.

PAUSE

Now, as you take a slow deep breath, and exhale slowly, this divinely guided light energy flows from your physical body into all your energy fields, filling your body and your energy fields with total peace.

Allow the Divine to integrate peace into your whole being—balancing, harmonizing, and healing—as you become an instrument of peace.

PAUSE

See and feel yourself moving among your family and friends, business associates, acquaintances, and friends you have yet to meet. Know they are drawn to your peaceful energy—in the same way a thirsty person in the desert is drawn to cool, clear water.

Know you are a fountain of peace for others.

PAUSE

As you maintain your connection with your divinity, through prayer and meditation—and as you walk in the light of peace with the people in your life—your interwoven light of peace flows into your community, your nation, and your world.

Take a few moments now to experience this brilliant light of peace, as it flows out from you and reaches everyone in your life and around the world.

PAUSE

Now allow the healing energy of peace to flow back to you.

PAUSE

As this divine light energy circles back to and through you, allow the healing energy of peace to go forth again and encircle Planet Earth and extend into the universe—divinely guided—into infinite space and then back to its home in your heart, and out again,

- in and out like the tide of the oceans,

- in and out with your breath.

PAUSE

Rest now in this healing energy of absolute peace for a few moments as you breathe in and out, in and out, in and out, in and out.

PAUSE

When you are ready to come out of meditation, count slowly from one to five. On the count of five, open your eyes and bring your awareness back to your physical reality.

One...two...three...four...five. Open your eyes and live in peace.

Sharing Peace

— Created by Rev. Claudell County, Unity School for Religious Studies

Get into a comfortable position with your feet flat on the floor and your back straight. Fully relax as you inhale and exhale several deep breaths. Focus your awareness just behind your eyes and slowly move your awareness down past your nose, your mouth, through your throat, and into your chest area. Hold your awareness at the level of your heart and feel the loving and peaceful energy of your heart.

Pause

Now imagine a golden cord of light emerging from your heart. Watch as it travels to the heart of the person nearest to you, perhaps in this room, perhaps in another room or in another building.

Let this golden cord of light continue to travel to your family members, your friends, your neighbors, the people where you shop, the people where you work, and the people on the highways.

Pause

As this golden cord of love reaches these people, know that it empowers the cords of love within them, which then begin to travel to the people in their lives. Let yourself hover above the matrix of love that is forming from the golden cords. See this matrix of love embrace your town, your state, your country, and the entire planet.

Pause

Observe the matrix of love embracing all people—bringing harmony, peace, and compassion to everyone. Witness people's hearts awakening, and their love reaching out farther and farther. See the earth completely covered in a matrix of golden light and love.

Pause

Watch as the rainforests begin to regenerate, areas of drought receive the blessing of rain, floods recede, and our planet is restored to wholeness. Feel the shift in energy as conflicts and wars cease, faith replaces all fear, and understanding and kindness return.

Peace reigns on earth.

PAUSE

Know that each person on the planet is safe, secure, and upheld by this love.

- We breathe easily.

- We are free from tensions and fears.

- We are at peace—open and receptive.

- We are surrendered in trust.

- We know there is love and only love and all is well.

PAUSE

When you choose to return, bring love and peace with you into this physical realm through your words and actions. Affirm: *I accept my responsibility to bring love and peace into my world, now. Thank you, Spirit.*

Mantra Meditation

– Adapted from Mantras & Mudra
by Lillian Too

Mantra: "OM MANI PADME HUM"

This is the most famous meditation mantra in the world. Many Buddhist practitioners chant it daily throughout their lives. It is the mantra of the Buddha of Compassion, known in Tibet as Buddha Chenrezig, in China as Kuan Yin, in India as Avalokiteshvara, and in Japan as Goddess Kwannon. It is said that reciting this mantra will help calm your fears, soothe your worries, answer your prayers, and lead you to heightened awareness, profound insights, and deep feelings of compassion. Repeat it over and over throughout your meditation.

193

Imagination is more important than knowledge.
Knowledge is limited. Imagination encircles the world.

– Albert Einstein

We have to transport our consciousness of America into the
future and imagine that which cannot be imagined, to recreate,
to summon new forms from the unknown, to draw forth new
structures which spring from higher awareness, a greater
understanding of ourselves, of our nation, and of the world.

– Congressman Dennis J. Kucinich

Guided Imagination Session on Peace

This section gives you step–by–step instructions for imagining peace. It is designed to help you imagine peace in your personal life, your community, your nation, or the world, depending on your focus. You may record the meditation for yourself or use it to guide others; it generally takes fifteen to twenty minutes. Be sure to make the natural and specified pauses long enough for the imagination to soar. Note that the headings are meant only to organize the session.

STEP 1: MERGING WITH THE LIGHT

Sit in a comfortable position with your feet flat on the floor and your back straight. Close your eyes and relax your body.

Take three deep breaths, holding them each for awhile and then breathing out completely as you deepen your relaxation.

PAUSE

Empty your mind and focus your attention gently on your breath. Note any thoughts or feelings that arise, without holding on to them. Just let them come and go. Relax and breathe naturally.

PAUSE

Imagine a pure white light filling your body, starting at the top of your head and slowly moving down through your head, neck, upper body and arms, midsection, legs, and feet. Feel yourself surrounded by and filled with pure white light, connecting you to divine consciousness above and to Mother Earth below.

Remain suspended in this light, where all is known and there is no time or space.

PAUSE

195

Ask the Divine, by whatever name you know it, to guide your experience in this session for the highest good for all concerned. Ask to remember whatever you are to know.

Feel yourself merging with the light. Know you are one with the light. Know you are one with all that is, including your highest desires and the divine plan for you.

STEP 2: Starting with Current Reality

From within the light, focus on a situation in your life or in the world that you are choosing to heal. Be aware of the current reality of this situation without judging it; just notice what it is like.

Pause

STEP 3: Imagining Peace—Level One

Now, expand your awareness to a point where the situation has been fully transformed, where the parties involved have fully realized peace. Without knowing how far ahead you are in time, and without knowing how it happened, just imagine that peace exists in this situation.

Rest and relax in this desired outcome. Be in the picture. Be one with peace.

- What is different around you?

- What is different within you?

- How are you expressing yourself?

Look around you and notice every detail:

- What colors, shapes, sounds, and smells do you notice?

- What can you touch?

- What are people saying to you and what do you say?

Fully feel what it is like to be at peace in this situation.

Pause

STEP 4: Imagining Peace—Level Two

Now, imagine that peace has existed in this situation for five years. Let your imagination leap forward in time, so that you are in this peaceful situation that has existed for five years.

- What is different now?

- What is different about you?

- How has your work changed?

- How has your life changed?

Just be in this consciousness and feel peace.

Pause

STEP 5: Imagining Peace—Level Three

Now, imagine you have been living in the consciousness of peace in this situation for ten more years.

- What's happening now?

- What's different in you?

- In what specific ways are you being an instrument of peace?

- With whom are you working?

- What are you co-creating?

Open yourself fully to experiencing the consciousness and activities of and from peace.

PAUSE

STEP 6: EXPANDING AND DEEPENING PEACE

Now expand and deepen your experience. Imagine someone you care for deeply is talking to you about the transformation that has occurred.

- What are they saying?

- What do you say?

- What are you feeling? Feel it. Let it permeate your body and mind.

Notice something near you that you can smell. Inhale deeply and let the fragrance permeate your being.

Reach out in your imagination and touch something or someone.

Enjoy your experience of oneness with this situation, with the experience of peace—from deep within yourself—feel an abiding gratitude for what has happened. Allow your gratitude for peace to fill your entire body. Feel gratitude for how far you have come, for who you are, and for what you have contributed to this peace.

Expand and deepen your gratitude even further.

PAUSE

STEP 7: REMEMBERING (OPTIONAL)

Now, remain within your consciousness of peace and remember back:

- What was the first thing that happened to create this peace?

- What was the most important change you made in your life to help bring about this peace?

From your peace consciousness, remember:

- What was the biggest obstacle to creating this peace?

- How was it overcome?

- What was the inner strength you relied on most?

STEP 8: SOAKING IN PEACE

Enjoy your peace consciousness. Ask for any additional information that is important for you to know and allow it to come to you.

PAUSE

STEP 9: RETURNING TO THE PRESENT

When you are ready, slowly come back to the present time and bring the consciousness of peace with you.

Open your eyes.

STEP 10: LIVING IN PEACE

Write down information you choose to remember from your imagination session. Recall and relive your peaceful consciousness often, holding loosely to the details and remaining in the *feeling* of peace and gratitude. In so doing, you allow for something even greater to occur.

One little person, giving all of her time to peace,

makes news. Many people, giving some of their time,

can make history.

— Peace Pilgrim

How wonderful it is that nobody need wait

a single moment before starting to improve the world.

— Anne Frank

We all can build bridges of love each day

With our eyes, our smiles, our touch

With our will to find a way

— Stephen Longfellow Fiske

Recommended Resources

This section offers you resources for expanding your understanding of the topics presented in *Ripples of Peace: 111 Ways You Can Help Create Peace in the World,* and for beginning your peace activities. They include hundreds of books, recordings, magazines, organizations, and Internet sites. You can find additional resources on the Web, by using keywords to search for your particular areas of interest, as well as in libraries and bookstores.

Books and Recordings

CONSCIOUSNESS

Allen, James, compiled by Laurel Creek Press. *The Wisdom of James Allen.* San Diego, CA: Laurel Creek Press, 2000.

Fox, Emmet. *Power Through Constructive Thinking.* New York: Harper San Francisco, a division of HarperCollins, 1989.

Hanh, Thich Nhat. *The Wisdom of Thich Nhat Hanh.* New York: One Spirit with Beacon Press and Parallax Press, 2000.

Holmes, Ernest. *The Science of Mind.* New York: Jeremy P. Tarcher/Putnam, a member of Penguin Putnam, Inc., 1966 with Foreword, 1997.

Hubbard, Barbara Marx. *Conscious Evolution: Awakening the Power of Our Social Potential.* Novato, CA: New World Library, 1998.

Krishnamurti, J. *Think on These Things.* New York: Harper & Row, 1964.

Levine, Stephen. *A Gradual Awakening.* Garden City, NY: Anchor Books, 1979.

Macy, Joanna and Thich Nhat Hanh. *World as Lover, World as Self.* Berkeley: Parallax Press, 1991.

McWilliams, Peter and John-Roger. *You Can't Afford the Luxury of a Negative Thought: A Book for People with Any Life-Threatening Illness—Including Life.* Los Angeles: Prelude Press, 1988.

Murphy, Joseph. *Collected Essays of Joseph Murphy*. Marina del Rey, CA: DeVorss & Company, 1990.

———*The Power of Your Subconscious Mind*. Englewood Cliffs, NJ: Prentice-Hall, Inc., 1963.

Neville. *Awakened Imagination*. Marina del Rey, CA: DeVorss & Company, 1954.

———*The Power of Awareness*. Marina del Rey, CA: DeVorss & Company, 1952, revised 1992.

Russell, Peter. *The Global Brain Awakens: Our Next Evolutionary Leap*. Palo Alto, CA: Global Brain, Inc., 1995.

Shinn, Florence Scovel. *The Game of Life and How to Play It*. New York: A Fireside Book by Simon & Schuster, 1925.

Shinn, Florence Scovel, compiled by Christine Schneider. *The Power of the Spoken Word*. Marina del Rey, CA: DeVorss & Company, 1945.

Talbot, Michael. *The Holographic Universe*. New York: HarperPerennial, a Division of HarperCollins*Publishers*, 1991.

Walsch, Neale Donald. *Conversations with God: Book 1*. New York: G.P. Putnam's Sons, 1995.

———*Conversations with God: Book 2*. Charlottesville, VA: Hampton Roads Publishing Company, Inc., 1997.

———*Conversations with God: Book 3*. Charlottesville, VA: Hampton Roads Publishing Company, Inc., 1998.

Walsch, Neale Donald and Brad Blanton. *Honest to God: A Change of Heart That Can Change the World*. Stanley, VA: Sparrowhawk Publications, 2002.

Wilber, Ken. *The Essential Ken Wilber: An Introductory Reader*. Boston: Shambhala, 1998.

———*The Spectrum of Consciousness*. Wheaton, IL: Quest Books, 1993, second edition.

Wolf, Fred Alan. *The Spiritual Universe: How Quantum Physics Proves the Existence of the Soul.* New York: Simon & Schuster, 1996.

Zukov, Gary. *The Dancing Wu Li Masters.* New York: Quill, William Morrow, 1979.

———*The Seat of the Soul.* New York: A Fireside Book published by Simon & Schuster, Inc., 1990.

Diversity, Conflict Resolution, and Unity

Capra, Fritjof. *The Web of Life: A New Scientific Understanding of Living Systems.* New York: Anchor Books, Doubleday, 1996.

Gingras Fitzell, Susan, ed. *Free the Children: Conflict Education for Strong, Peaceful Minds.* Gabriola Island, British Columbia, Canada: New Society Publishers, 1997.

Hanh, Thich Nhat. *Anger: Wisdom for Cooling the Flames.* New York: Riverhead Books, 2001.

Leach, Joy with Bette George, Tina Jackson, and Arleen LaBella. *A Practical Guide to Working with Diversity: The Process, the Tools, the Resources.* New York: Amacom, 1995.

Lemkow, Anna F. *The Wholeness Principle: Dynamics of Unity Within Science, Religion & Society.* Wheaton, IL: Quest Books, 1990.

Lerner, Harriet. *The Dance of Connection: How to Talk to Someone When You're Mad, Hurt, Scared, Frustrated, Insulted, Betrayed, or Desperate.* New York: Harper CollinsPublishers, 2001.

Lieberman, David J. *Make Peace With Anyone: Breakthrough Strategies to Quickly End Any Conflict, Feud, or Estrangement.* New York: St. Martin's Press, 2002.

Mayer, Bernard S. *The Dynamics of Conflict Resolution: A Practitioner's Guide.* San Francisco: Jossey-Bass, 2000.

Saunders, Harold H. *A Public Peace Process: Sustained Dialogue to Transform Racial and Ethnic Conflicts.* New York: Palgrave Macmillan, 2001.

203

FAITH TRADITIONS AND SPIRITUALITY

Anderson, Sherry Ruth and Patricia Hopkins. *The Feminine Face of God: The Unfolding of the Sacred in Women.* New York: Bantam Books, 1992.

Arberry, A.J. *The Koran Interpreted.* New York: A Touchstone Book, published by Simon & Schuster, 1955.

Beliefnet. *From the Ashes: A Spiritual Response to the Attack on America.* United States: Rodale, Inc. and Beliefnet, Inc., 2001.

Brussat, Frederic and Mary Ann. *Spiritual Literacy: Reading the Sacred in Everyday Life.* New York: Scribner, 1996.

Chopra, Deepak. *How to Know God: The Soul's Journey into the Mystery of Mysteries.* New York: Three Rivers Press, 2000.

Das, Lama Surya. *Awakening the Buddha Within: Tibetan Wisdom for the Western World.* New York: Broadway Books, 1997.

Foundation for Inner Peace. *A Course in Miracles.* Tiburon, CA: Foundation for Inner Peace, 1985.

Dyer, Wayne. *There's a Spiritual Solution to Every Problem.* New York: Harper CollinsPublishers, 2001.

Harlow, Rabbi Jules, ed. *Mahzor for Rosh Hashanah and Yom Kippur: A Prayer Book for the Days of Awe.* New York: The Rabbinical Assembly, 1989.

Labowitz, Rabbi Shoni. *Miraculous Living: A Guided Journey in Kabbalah Through the Ten Gates of the Tree of Life.* New York: A Fireside Book, published by Simon & Schuster, 1996.

Light of Truth Universal Shrine. *Truth is One Paths are Many.* Yogaville, VA: Integral Yoga Publications, 1989.

Linssen, Robert. *Living Zen.* New York: Grove Press, Inc., 1958, reprinted in 1978.

204

McGaa, Ed. *Mother Earth Spirituality: Native American Paths to Healing Ourselves and the World*. San Francisco: Harper & Row, 1990.

Muller, Wayne. *Touching the Divine* (audio). Boulder, CO: Sounds True Audio, 1994.

Parfitt, Will. *The New Living Qabalah: A Practical & Experiential Guide to Understanding the Tree of Life*. Shaftesbury, Dorset: Element, 1995.

Parrinder, Geoffrey, compiler. *The Wisdom of Jesus*. Oxford: Oneworld Publications, 2000.

Pope John Paul II. *The Private Prayers of Pope John Paul II*. New York: Pocket Books, 2001.

Rinpoche, Sogyal. *Glimpse After Glimpse: Daily Reflections on Living and Dying*. New York: HarperSanFrancisco, A Division of HarperCollins*Publishers*, 1995.

———*The Tibetan Book of Living and Dying*. New York: HarperSanFrancisco, A Division of HarperCollins*Publishers*, 1992.

Rozak, Theodore. *The Voice of the Earth*. New York: Simon & Schuster, 1992.

Shah, Idries. *The Sufis*. Garden City, NY: Anchor Books, Doubleday & Company, Inc., 1971.

Smith, Huston. *The World's Religions*. New York: HarperSanFrancisco, 1991.

Sri Swami Satchidananda. *The Golden Present: Daily Inspirational Readings*. Yogaville, VA: Integral Yoga Publications, 1987.

———*The Living Gita: The Complete Bhagavad Gita*. Yogaville, VA: Integral Yoga Publications, 1988.

The Holy Bible, Revised Standard Version. Toronto: Thomas Nelson & Sons, 1952.

Wilhelm, Richard, translator. *The Secret of the Golden Flower: A Chinese Book of Life*. San Diego, CA: A Harvest/HBJ Book, A Helen and Kurt Wolff Book, published by Harcourt Brace Jovanovich, 1931, revised 1962.

Beattie, Melody. *Choices: Taking Control of Your Life and Making It Matter*. New York: HarperSanFrancisco, a Division of HarperCollins*Publishers*, 2002.

Belitz, Charlene and Meg Lundstrom. *The Power of Flow: Practical Ways to Transform Your Life with Meaningful Coincidence*. New York: Harmony Books, 1997.

Bennett–Goleman, Tara. *Emotional Alchemy: How the Mind Can Heal the Heart*. New York: Three Rivers Press, 2001.

Borysenko, Joan. *Inner Peace for Busy People: 52 Simple Strategies for Transforming Your Life*. Carlsbad, CA: Hay House, Inc., 2001.

———*The Power of the Mind to Heal: Renewing Body, Mind, and Spirit* (audio). Niles, IL: Nightingale Conant, 1998.

Breathnach, Sarah Ban. *Simple Abundance: A Daybook of Comfort and Joy*. New York: Warner Books, Inc., a Time Warner Company, 1995.

———*Simple Abundance Journal of Gratitude*. New York: Warner Books, Inc., a Time Warner Company, 1996.

Childre, Doc and Howard Martin with Donna Beech. *The Heartmath Solution*. New York: HarperSanFrancisco, a Division of HarperCollins*Publishers*, 1999.

Chödrön, Pema. *The Places That Scare You: A Guide to Fearlessness in Difficult Times*. Boston: Shambhala Publications, Inc., 2001.

———*When Things Fall Apart: Heart Advice for Difficult Times*. Boston: Shambhala Publications, Inc., 1997.

Dominguez, Joe and Vicki Robin. *Your Money or Your Life*. New York: Penguin, 1993.

Dreher, Diane. *The Tao of Inner Peace*. New York: A Plume Book published by the Penguin Group, 2000.

Dychtwald, Ken. *Bodymind*. Los Angeles: Jeremy P. Tarcher, Inc., 1977.

Fritz, Robert. *The Path of Least Resistance: Learning to Become the Creative Force in Your Own Life*. New York: Fawcett Columbine, 1989.

Gawain, Shakti with Laurel King. *Living in the Light: A Guide to Personal and Planetary Transformation*. Mill Valley, CA: Whatever Publishing, Inc., 1986.

Goldberg, Philip. *The Intuitive Edge: Understanding Intuition and Applying It in Everyday Life*. Los Angeles: Jeremy P. Tarcher, Inc., 1983.

Goleman, Daniel. *Emotional Intelligence*. New York: Bantam Books, 1995.

Hanh, Thich Nhat. *Being Peace*. Berkeley: Parallax Press, 1987.

Lesser, Elizabeth. *The Seeker's Guide: Making Your Life a Spiritual Adventure*. New York: Villard, 1999.

Loeb, Paul Rogat. *Soul of a Citizen: Living with Conviction in a Cynical Time*. New York: St. Martin's Griffin, 1999.

Luhrs, Janet. *The Simple Living Guide: A Sourcebook for Less Stressful, More Joyful Living*. New York: Broadway Books, 1997.

Moore, Thomas. *Care of the Soul*. New York: HarperCollins*Publishers*, 1992.

Mountain Dreamer, Oriah. *The Invitation*. New York: HarperCollins and HarperSanFrancisco, 1999.

Rabbin, Robert. *The Sacred Hub: Living in Our Real Self*. San Francisco: Inner Directions Foundation, 1996.

Rabinowitz, Ilana. *Mountains are Mountains and Rivers are Rivers: Applying Eastern Teachings to Everyday Life*. New York: Hyperion, 1999.

Ruiz, Don Miguel. *The Four Agreements: A Practical Guide to Personal Freedom*. San Rafael, CA: Amber–Allen Publishing, 1997.

Russell, Peter. *Waking Up in Time: Finding Inner Peace in Times of Accelerating Change*. Novato, CA: Origin Press, 1992.

Ryan, M.J. *Attitudes of Gratitude: How to Give and Receive Joy Every Day of Your Life*. Berkeley, CA: Conari Press, 1999.

Schaef, Anne Wilson. *Beyond Therapy, Beyond Science: A New Model for Healing the Whole Person*. New York: HarperSanFrancisco, a division of HarperCollins*Publishers*, 1992.

———*Living in Process: Basic Truths for Living the Path of Soul*. New York: Ballantine Wellspring, 1998.

Seaward, Brian Luke. *Stand Like Mountain Flow Like Water: Reflections on Stress and Human Spirituality*. Deerfield Beach, FL: Health Communications, Inc., 1997.

The Dalai Lama and Howard C. Cutler. *The Art of Happiness*. New York: Riverhead Books, a member of Penguin Putnam, Inc., 1998.

The Dalai Lama, with Frédérique Hatier. *The Spirit of Peace: Teachings on Love, Compassion and Everyday Life*. New York: HarperCollins*Publishers*, 2002.

Tolle, Eckhart. *The Power of Now: A Guide to Spiritual Enlightenment*. Novato, CA: New World Library, 1999.

Zweig, Connie and Jeremiah Abrams, eds. *Meeting the Shadow: The Hidden Power of the Dark Side of Human Nature*. New York: Jeremy P. Tarcher/Putnam Book published by G.P. Putnam's Sons, 1991.

Zweig, Connie and Steve Wolf. *Romancing the Shadow: Illuminating the Dark Side of the Soul*. New York: Ballantine Books, 1997.

LOVE AND SERVICE

Barrows, Anita and Joanna Macy, translators. *Rilke's Book of Hours: Love Poems to God*. New York: Riverhead Books, published by The Berkley Publishing Group, a member of Putnam Penguin, Inc., 1996.

Braybrooke, Marcus, ed. *Life Lines*. London: Duncan Baird Publishers, 2002.

Greenleaf, Robert. *Servant Leadership*. Mahwah, NJ: Paulist Press, 1977.

Helminski, Kabir. *The Rumi Collection*. Boston: Shambhala Publications, 2000.

Keyes, Ken Jr. *The Power of Unconditional Love.* Coos Bay, OR: Love Line Books, 1990.

Luks, Allan with Peggy Payne. *The Healing Power of Doing Good.* New York: Ballantine Books, 1991.

Salzberg, Sharon. *Lovingkindness: The Revolutionary Art of Happiness.* Boston: Shambhala Publications, 1995.

Schulz, William F. *In Our Own Best Interest: How Defending Human Rights Benefits Us All.* Boston: Beacon Press, 2002.

The Dalai Lama and Howard C. Cutler. *Ethics for the New Millennium.* New York: Riverhead Books, published by The Berkley Publishing Group, a division of Penguin Putnam, Inc., 1999.

Trout, Susan S. *Born to Serve: The Evolution of the Soul Through Service.* Washington, DC: Three Roses Press, 1997.

————*To See Differently: Personal Growth and Being of Service Through Attitudinal Healing.* Washington, DC: Three Roses Press, 1990.

MEDITATION AND PRAYER

Beattie, Melody. *The Language of Letting Go: Daily Meditations for Codependents.* New York: A Hazelden Book, HarperCollins*Publishers*, 1990.

Braybrooke, Marcus. *Learn to Pray.* San Francisco: Chronicle Books, 2001.

Brunton, Paul. *Advanced Contemplation: The Peace Within You.* Burdett, NY: Larson Publications, 1988.

Dunn, Philip. *Prayer: Language of the Soul.* New York: Daybreak Books, an imprint of Rodale Books, 1997.

Easwaren, Eknath. *Meditation.* Tornales, CA: Nilgiri Press, 1991.

Goldstein, Joseph. *Insight Meditation: The Practice of Freedom.* Boston: Shambhala Publications, Inc., 1994.

Hanh, Thich Nhat. *For a Future to Be Possible: Commentaries on the Five Mindfulness Trainings*. Berkeley, CA: Parallax Press, 1993.

Kabat-Zinn, Jon. *Wherever You Go There You Are: Mindfulness Meditation in Everyday Life*. New York: Hyperion, 1994.

Kornfield, Jack. *The Art of Forgiveness, Lovingkindness, and Peace*. New York: Bantam Books, 2002.

LeShan, Lawrence. *How to Meditate*. Toronto: Bantam Books, 1974.

Moore, Thomas. *Meditations*. New York: Harper Collins*Publishers*, 1994.

Mother Teresa, edited by Becky Benenate. *In the Heart of the World: Thoughts, Stories, & Prayers*. Novato, CA: New World Library, 1997.

Ruiz, Don Miguel. *Prayers: A Communion with Our Creator*. San Rafael, CA: Amber-Allen Publishing, 2001.

Spangler, David. *Blessing: The Art and the Practice*. New York: Riverhead Books, a member of Penguin Putnam, Inc., 2001.

Stanley, Charles. *A Touch of Peace: Meditations on Experiencing the Peace of God*. Grand Rapids, MI: Zondervan Publishing House, 1993.

Summer Rain, Mary. *Whispered Wisdom: Portraits of Grandmother Earth*. Norfolk, VA: Hampton Roads Publishing Company, Inc., 1992.

Too, Lillian. *Mantras & Mudras: Meditations for the Hands and Voice to Bring Peace and Inner Calm*. London: HarperCollins*Publishers*, 2002.

Williamson, Marianne. *Illuminata: Thoughts, Prayers, Rites of Passage*. New York: Random House, 1994.

"Words of Inner Peace." *Natural Health*, December 2001.

NONVIOLENCE AND SOCIAL CHANGE

Ansbro, John J. *Martin Luther King, Jr.: Nonviolent Strategies and Tactics for Social Change*. Lanham, MD: Madison Books, Inc., 2000.

Attenborough, Richard, compiler. *The Words of Gandhi*. New York: Newmarket Press, 2000.

Beacon Press. *The Power of Nonviolence: Writings by Advocates of Peace*. Boston: Beacon Press, 2002.

Bobo, Kimberly, Jacqueline A. Kendall, and Steve Max. *Organizing for Social Change*. Santa Ana, CA: Seven Locks Press, 1990.

Breton, Denise and Christopher Largent. *The Paradigm Conspiracy: Why Our Social Systems Violate Human Potential and How We Can Change Them*. Center City, MN: Hazeldon, 1996.

Carson, Clayborne, ed. *The Autobiography of Martin Luther King, Jr.* New York: Warner Books, 1998.

Chadha, Yogesh. *Gandhi: A Life*. New York: John Wiley & Sons, Inc., 1997.

Gandhi, Mohandas K. *Autobiography: The Story of My Experiments with Truth*. New York: Dover Publications, Inc., 1983.

———*Nonviolent Resistance*. New York: Shocken Books, 1951.

Hahn, Thich Nhat. *Love in Action: Writings on Nonviolent Social Change*. Berkeley, CA: Parallax Press, 1993.

Harman, Willis. *Global Mind Change: The Promise of the 21st Century*. San Francisco: Berrett–Koehler in cooperation with the Institute of Noetic Sciences, 1998.

Horwitz, Claudia. *The Spiritual Activist: Practices to Transform Your Life, Your Work, and Your World*. New York: Penguin Compass, published by the Penguin Group, 2002.

Houston, Jean. *Jump Time: Shaping Your Future in a World of Radical Change*. New York: Jeremy P. Tarcher/Putnam, a member of Penguin Putnam, Inc., 2000.

McLaughlin, Corinne and Gordon Davidson. *Spiritual Politics: Changing the World from the Inside Out*. New York: Ballantine Books, 1994.

Prokosch, Mike and Laura Raymond, eds. *The Global Activist's Manual: Local Ways to Change the World*. New York: Thunder's Mouth Press/Nation Books, 2002.

Ray, Paul H. and Sherry Ruth Anderson. *The Cultural Creatives: How 50 Million People are Changing the World*. New York: Harmony Books, 2000.

Ryan, M.J. ed. *The Fabric of the Future*. Berkeley, CA: Conari Press, 1998.

Schaef, Anne Wilson. *When Society Becomes an Addict*. New York: Harper & Row, 1988.

Wallis, Jim. *The Soul of Politics*. New York: Orbis Press/The New Press, 1994.

Williamson, Marianne. *Healing the Soul of America: Reclaiming Our Voices as Spiritual Citizens*. New York: A Touchstone Book, published by Simon & Schuster, 2000.

———*Imagine: What America Could Be in the 21st Century*. United States: Rodale, Inc., 2000.

Wink, Walter, ed., and the Fellowship of Reconciliation and Richard Deats. *Peace is the Way: Writings on Nonviolence from the Fellowship of Reconciliation*. Maryknoll, NY: Orbis Books, 2000.

PEACE AT WORK

Autry, James A. *Love and Profit: The Art of Caring Leadership*. New York: Avon Books, 1991.

Block, Peter. *Stewardship: Choosing Service Over Self-Interest*. San Francisco: Berrett–Koehler Publishers, 1993.

Covey, Stephen R. *Principle-Centered Leadership*. New York: A Fireside Book, published by Simon & Schuster, 1991.

Ellinor, Linda. *Dialogue: Rediscover the Transforming Power of Conversation*. New York: John Wiley & Sons, 1998.

Hawley, Jack. *Reawakening the Spirit In Work: The Power of Dharmic Management*. San Francisco: Berrett–Koehler Publishers, 1993.

Rabbin, Robert. *Igniting the Soul at Work: A Mandate for Mystics*. Charlottesville, VA: Hampton Roads Publishing, 2002.

Renesch, John, ed. *New Traditions in Business: Spirit and Leadership in the 21st Century*. San Francisco: Berrett–Koehler Publishers, 1992.

Rosen, Robert, Patricia Digh, Marshall Singer, and Carl Phillips. *Global Literacies: Lessons on Business Leadership and National Cultures*. New York: Simon & Schuster, 2000.

Toms, Michael and Justine Willis Toms. *True Work: Doing What You Love and Loving What You Do*. New York: Three Rivers Press, 1999.

Weisbord, Marvin R. *Discovering Common Ground*. San Francisco: Berrett–Koehler Publishers, 1992.

Whyte, David. *The Heart Aroused: Poetry and the Preservation of the Soul in Corporate America*. New York: Currency/Doubleday, 1994.

215

Whitmyer, Claude, ed. *Mindfulness and Meaningful Work: Explorations in Right Livelihood*. Berkeley, CA: Parallax Press, 1994.

PEACEFUL RELATIONSHIPS AND COMMUNITIES

Eisler, Riane. *The Partnership Way: New Tools for Living and Learning, Healing Our Families, Our Communities, and Our World*. New York: HarperSanFrancisco, a division of HarperCollins*Publishers*, 1990.

Kasl, Charlotte Sophia. *A Home for the Heart*. New York: HarperPerennial, a division of HarperCollins*Publishers*, 1998.

Levine, Stephen and Ondrea. *Embracing the Beloved: Relationship as a Path of Awakening*. New York: Anchor Books, Doubleday, 1977.

Peck, M. Scott. *The Different Drum: Community Making and Peace*. New York: A Touchstone Book, published by Simon & Schuster, Inc., 1987.

Rosenberg, Marshall B. *Nonviolent Communication: A Language of Compassion*. PuddleDancer Press, 1999.

Stone, Douglas and Bruce Patton, Sheila Heen, and Roger Foster. *Difficult Conversations: How to Discuss What Matters Most.* New York: Penguin USA, 2000.

Taylor-Ide, Daniel and Carl E. Taylor. *Just and Lasting Change: When Communities Own Their Futures.* Baltimore, MD: The Johns Hopkins University Press in association with Future Generations, 2002.

Welwood, John. *Journey of the Heart: Intimate Relationship and the Path of Love.* New York: HarperCollins*Publishers*, 1990.

Tools and Techniques

Brown, Simon. *Practical Feng Shui.* London: Ward Lock, 1997.

Buzan, Tony with Barry Buzan. *The Mind Map Book.* New York: Dutton, published by the Penguin Group, 1993.

Campbell, Don. *The Mozart Effect: Tapping the Power of Music to Heal the Body, Strengthen the Mind, and Unlock the Creative Spirit.* New York: Avon Books, 1997.

Hale, Gill. *The Practical Encyclopedia of Feng Shui.* London: Hermes House, an imprint of Anness Publishing Limited, 2001.

Hittleman, Richard. *Richard Hittleman's Yoga: 28 Day Exercise Plan.* New York: Workman Publishing Company, 1969.

Linn, Denise. *Sacred Space: Clearing and Enhancing the Energy of Your Home.* New York: Ballantine Books, 1995.

Miles, Elizabeth. *Tune Your Brain: Using Music to Manage Your Mind, Body, and Mood.* New York: Berkley Books, 1997.

Poplawski, Thomas. *Eurythmy: Rhythm, Dance and Soul (Rudolf Steiner's Ideas in Practice Series).* Herndon, VA: Anthroposophic Press, 1998.

World Peace

Abdullah, Sharif. *Creating a World That Works for All.* San Francisco: Berrett-Koehler Publishers, Inc., 1999.

Diamond, Louise. *The Courage for Peace: Daring to Create Harmony in Ourselves and the World*. Berkeley, CA: Conari Press, 2000.

——*The Peace Book: 108 Simple Ways to Create a More Peaceful World*. Berkeley, CA: Conari Press, 2001.

Diamond, Louise and John W. MacDonald. *Multi-Track Diplomacy: A Systems Approach to Peace*. West Hartford, CT: Kumarian Press, 1996.

Donnelly, Doris. *Forgiveness and Peacemaking*. Erie, PA: Benet Press, 1993.

Epperly, Bruce G. and Rabbi Lewis Solomon. *Mending The World: Special Hope for Ourselves and Our Planet*. Philadelphia: Innisfree Press, Inc., 2002.

Fiske, Stephen Longfellow. *The Art of Peace: A Personal Manual on Peacemaking and Creativity*. Pasadena, CA: New Paradigm Books, 1995.

Helmick, Raymond G. and Rodney Lawrence Peterson, eds., and Desmond Mpilo Tutu. *Forgiveness and Reconciliation: Religion, Public Policy and Conflict Transformation*. Chicago: Templeton Foundation Press, 2001.

Houston, Jean. *Manual for the Peacemaker*. Wheaton, IL: Quest Books, 1995.

Ikeda, Daisaku. *For the Sake of Peace: Seven Paths to Global Harmony—A Buddhist Perspective*. Santa Monica, CA: Middleway Press, a division of the SGI–USA, 2002.

Jampolsky, Lee. *Healing Together: How to Bring Peace into Your Life and the World*. Hoboken, NJ: John Wiley & Sons, 2002.

Kierman, Anna, ed. *Voices for Peace: An Anthology*. London: Scribner, an imprint of Simon & Schuster UK Ltd., 2001.

Oates, Robert M. *Permanent Peace: How to Stop Terrorism and War—Now and Forever*. Fairfield, IA: Institute of Science, Technology and Public Policy, 2002.

Sri Swami Satchidananda. *Pathways to Peace*. Yogaville, VA: Integral Yoga Publications, 1988.

Periodicals

Hope
P.O. Box 52242
Boulder, CO 80323
(800) 513-0869
www.hopemag.com

In These Times
2040 N. Milwaukee Avenue
Chicago, IL 60647
(800) 827-0270
www.inthesetimes.com

Mother Jones
P.O. Box 469024
Escondido, CA 94046
(800) 334-8152
www.motherjones.com

IONS Review
101 San Antonio Road
Petaluma, CA 94952
(707) 775-3500
www.noetic.org

Science of Mind
P.O. Box 18087
Anaheim, CA 92817
(800) 247-6463
www.scienceofmind.com

Spirituality and Health
74 Trinity Place
New York, NY 10006
(212) 602-0705
www.spiritualityhealth.com

The Green Money Journal
P.O. Box 67
Santa Fe, NM 87504
(505) 988-7423
www.greenmoney.com

Tikkun
26 Fell Street
San Francisco, CA 94102
(800) 395-7753
www.tikkun.org

Utne Reader
P.O. Box 7460
Red Oak, IA 51591
(800) 736-8863
www.utne.com

YES!
Positive Futures Network
P.O. Box 10818
Bainbridge Island, WA 98110
(800) 937-4451
www.yesmagazine.org

Organizations and Internet Sites

A Conflict Resolution Page

An Internet resource that provides extensive links to web sites related to conflict resolution

http://www.geocities.com/Athens/8945/links.html

Albert Schweitzer Institute for the Humanities

Nonprofit, nonpartisan, nongovernmental institute affiliated with the United Nations that helps to sustain reverence for life by supporting educational, spiritual, and physical well-being within humanity and the environment

515 Sherman Avenue
Hamden, CT 06514
(203) 562-3039

American Friends Service Committee

Quaker organization that includes people of various faiths who are committed to social justice, peace, and humanitarian service

1501 Cherry Street
Philadelphia, PA 19102
(215) 241-7000
www.afsc.org

Amnesty International

Nobel Prize–winning activist organization dedicated to freeing prisoners of conscience, gaining fair trials for political prisoners, ending torture, political killings and "disappearances," and abolishing the death penalty

322 Eighth Avenue, 10th Floor
New York, NY 10001
(212) 807-8400

www.aiusa.org

Art of Living Foundation

International nongovernmental organization that provides education to individuals in order to eliminate stress, create a sense of belonging, restore human values, and encourage celebration and service

www.artofliving.org

Association for Humanistic Psychology

Group committed to holistic and interdisciplinary research and practices that contribute to understanding, developing, and nurturing unrealized human potential, as well as a more conscious and humane global society

1516 Oak Street, #320A
Alameda, CA 94501-2947
(510) 769-6495

http://ahpweb.org/involve/resources.html

Business for Social Responsibility

Global nonprofit organization that helps member companies achieve commercial success in ways that respect people, communities, ethical values, and the environment

111 Sutter Street, 12th Floor
San Francisco, CA 94104
(415) 984-3200
www.bsr.org

Center for Nonviolent Communication

Global organization helping people compassionately connect with one another and themselves through a specific process of nonviolent communication

2428 Foothill Boulevard, Suite E
La Crescenta, CA 91214
(818) 957-9393
www.cnvc.org

Center for Visionary Leadership

Organization that helps people develop the inner resources to be effective leaders and respond creatively to change

West Coast
369 Third Street, #563
San Rafael, CA 94901
(415) 847-4989
www.visionarylead.org

East Coast
P.O. Box 2241
Arlington, VA 22202
(202) 237-2800

CHILDREACH

U.S. member of PLAN International that matches sponsors to children around the world to meet the children's basic human needs and help them achieve economic and social betterment

155 Plan Way
Warwick, RI 02886
(800) 556-7918
www.childreach.org

CHILDREN INTERNATIONAL

Organization that coordinates delivery of health care, education, food and vitamins, and clothing through contributing sponsors to improve the lives of children around the world

2000 East Red Bridge
P.O. Box 219055
Kansas City, MO 64121
(800) 888-3089
www.children.org

CITIZENS FOR INDEPENDENT PUBLIC BROADCASTING

National membership organization that works for an independently funded, accountable, truly public broadcasting system

901 Old Hickory Road
Pittsburgh, PA 15243
(412) 341-1967
www.cipbonline.org

Conflict Resolution Consortium

A multidisciplinary program of research, teaching, and application that focuses on finding constructive ways of addressing difficult, long-term, and intractable conflicts

www.colorado.edu/conflict

Co-op America

Organization dedicated to creating a just and sustainable society by harnessing economic power and working with both consumer and business sides of the equation

1612 K Street NW, Suite 600
Washington, DC 20006
(800) 584-7336

www.coopamerica.org

Department of Peace (HR 2459)

Bill introduced to the United States House of Representatives by Congressman Dennis Kucinich to make nonviolence an organizing principle in our society, to help create peace in homes, families, schools, neighborhoods, cities, and the nation, as well as worldwide

www.dopcampaign.org

Doctors Without Borders

Group that delivers emergency aid to victims of armed conflict, natural and man-made disasters, and epidemics; and to others who lack health care because of social or geographical isolation

333 7th Avenue, 2nd Floor
New York, NY 10001–5004
(212) 679–6800
www.doctorswithoutborders.org

Earth Charter Community Summits

Grassroots efforts to bring people together in cities around the world in support of the Earth Charter, a declaration of interdependence

www.earthchartersummits.org
www.earthcharter.org

Economic Policy Institute

Nonprofit, nonpartisan think tank that seeks to broaden the public debate about strategies to achieve a prosperous and fair economy

1660 L Street NW, Suite 1200
Washington, DC 20036
(202) 775–8810
www.epinet.org

Emissary of Light

Web site based on the work of troubador James Twyman, including prayers for peace, concert schedules, and related courses and products

www.emissaryoflight.com

FAIR

National media watch group that offers well-documented criticism of media bias and censorship and advocates for greater diversity in the press

112 W. 27th Street
New York, NY 10001
(212) 633-6700

www.fair.org

Fellowship of Reconciliation

Largest and oldest interfaith peace organization in the United States, committed to active nonviolence as a transforming way of life through nonviolence training, religious peace fellowships, and other peace programs

521 N. Broadway
Nyack, NY 10960
(845) 358-4601

www.forusa.org
www.forusa.org/Interfaith/rpfs.html

Foundation for International Community Assistance

Organization that provides destitute mothers with small loans to enable them to start or expand small businesses and become self-sufficient

1101 14th Street NW
Washington, DC 20005
(202) 682-1510
www.villagebanking.org

Friends of the Earth

Group that documents and opposes environmental destruction by transnational companies

1025 Vermont Avenue NW, Suite 300
Washington, DC 20005
(877) 843-8687

www.foe.org

Global Renaissance Alliance

Organization that supports information exchange and ways to move from fear to love, including the formation of peace circles, as a way to heal the world

P.O. Box 3259
Center Line, MI 48015
(586) 754-8105

www.renaissancealliance.org

Greenpeace USA

Independent organization that uses nonviolent confrontation to expose environmental problems and bring about solutions for a green/peaceful future

702 H Street NW, Suite 300
Washington, DC 20001
(202) 462-1177

www.greenpeace.org

Habitat for Humanity

International organization that brings families and communities in need together with volunteers and resources to build decent, affordable housing

Partner Service Center
121 Habitat Street
Americus, GA 31709-3498
(229) 924-6935, ext. 2551 or 2552

www.habitat.org

Human Rights Watch

Independent, nongovernmental organization dedicated to protecting the human rights of people around the world

350 Fifth Avenue, 34th Floor
New York, NY 10118-3299
(212) 290-4700

www.hrw.org

Hunger Project

Strategic organization and global movement committed to ending hunger

15 East 26th Street
New York, NY 10010
(212) 251-9100
www.thp.org

Institute for Peace and Justice

Independent, interfaith, nonprofit organization committed to working for justice as the means to peace

4144 Lindell Boulevard #408
St. Louis, MO 63108
(314) 533-4445
www.ipj-ppj.org

Institute for Public Accuracy

Group that seeks to broaden public discourse by gaining media access for those whose perspectives are commonly drowned out by corporate-backed think tanks and other influential institutions

65 Ninth Street, Suite 3
San Francisco, CA 94103
(415) 552-5378
www.accuracy.org

Organizations and Internet Sites

Institute for the Advancement of Service

Nonprofit educational and spiritual organization that focuses on the practice of service and the care of the self

P.O. Box 19222
Alexandria, VA 22320
(703) 706-5333
www.ias-online.org

Institute for Multi-Track Diplomacy

Group that promotes a transformative, systems approach to peace in places of deep-rooted conflict around the world

1925 North Lynn Street, 12th Floor
Arlington, VA 22209
(703) 528-3863
www.imtd.org

Institute of Noetic Sciences

Nonprofit membership organization that conducts and sponsors research into the workings and powers of the mind

101 San Antonio Road
Petaluma, CA 94952
(707) 775-3500
www.noetic.org

INTERNATIONAL DAY OF PEACE

Designated as September 21 by the United Nations General Assembly

www.peaceoneday.org

INTERNATIONAL NETWORK FOR THE DANCES OF UNIVERSAL PEACE

The coordinating hub that links the dance circles, based on the timeless tradition of sacred dance, worldwide

6310 NE 7th Street, Suite 209E
Seattle, WA 98115
www.dancesofuniversalpeace.org

INTERNATIONAL RESCUE COMMITTEE

Nonsectarian organization that provides relief, protection, and resettlement services for refugees and victims of oppression and violent conflict

122 East 42nd Street
New York, NY 10168-1289
(212) 551-3000
www.theIRC.org

Kirkridge Retreat Center

Christian center with an ecumenical spirit that provides a place for spiritual renewal and conducts programs emphasizing the cultivation of a deep spirituality to sustain compassionate action

2495 Fox Gap Road
Bangor, PA 18013–6028
(610) 588–1793
www.kirkridge.org

Life Foundation

International organization that provides service to society through spiritual disciplines, courses and retreats, dru yoga, detraumatization programs, and world peace flames

www.lifefoundation.org.uk

Lightshift

Network of people using collaborative meditation to help shift the consciousness in the world toward love, joy, and peace

www.lightshift.com

Meditation Society of America

Web site that provides information and links to more than 100 meditation techniques

www.meditationsociety.com

MoveOn

Nationwide on-line network of more than one million activists committed to broadening citizen participation to counter the influence of monied interests and partisan extremes

www.moveon.org

New Dimensions World Broadcasting Network

Independent producer of broadcast dialogues and programming on views from many traditions and cultures, aiming to foster healthy lives and a deep connection to self, family, community, the natural world, and the planet

P.O. Box 569
Ukiah, CA 95482
(707) 468–5215

www.newdimensions.org

Nuclear Age Peace Foundation

Organization committed to eliminating nuclear weapons and building a legacy of peace through education and advocacy

PMB 121, 1187 Coast Village Road, Suite 1
Santa Barbara, CA 93108
(805) 965–3443

www.wagingpeace.org

ONE WORLD

Community of more than 1,250 organizations working for social justice

17th Floor, 89 Albert Embankment
London SE1 7TP, United Kingdom
44 (0)20 7735 2100

www.oneworld.net

OXFAM AMERICA

Organization that works with poor communities around the world to solve problems of hunger, poverty, and social injustice

26 West Street
Boston, MA 02111
(800) 776-9326

www.oxfamamerica.org

PEACE ACTION

Membership organization that works to abolish nuclear weapons, redirect excessive Pentagon spending to domestic investments, end global weapon sales, and resolve international conflicts peacefully

1100 Wayne Avenue, Suite 1020
Silver Spring, MD 20910
(301) 565-4050

www.peace-action.org

Peace Brigades International

Group that offers unarmed protective accompaniment to people, organizations, and communities threatened by violence and human rights abuses

428 8th Street SE, 2nd Floor
Washington, DC 20003
(202) 544-3765
www.igc.apc.org/pbi/usa.html

Peace Village

New York site that offers weekend retreats and a place for spiritual renewal

O'Hara Road, Route 23A
Haines Falls, NY 12436
(518) 589-5000
www.peacevillage.com

Peaceweb

Quaker web page on peace and social concerns

www.quaker.org/peaceweb

PeaceWorks

Not-only-for-profit American company that promotes peace through business

www.peaceworks.com

PeaceWorkers

Civilian Peace Service in the United Kingdom through which people of all ages and backgrounds can participate in international civilian peacekeeping, peacemaking and peacebuilding missions

www.peaceworkers.org.uk

Points of Light Foundation

National, nonpartisan, nonprofit organization that promotes volunteerism in partnership with the Volunteer Center National Network

1400 I Street NW, Suite 800
Washington, DC 20005
(202) 729–8000
www.pointsoflight.org

Prayer Vigil for the Earth

Vigil held each September on the grounds of the Washington Monument in Washington, DC., as a living prayer for harmony and peace

www.oneprayer.org

Rainforest Action Network

Group working to protect tropical rainforests and human rights of nearby people

221 Pine Street, #500
San Francisco, CA 94104
(415) 398-4404
www.ran.org

Resources for Peace

Organization that provides links to web sites related to peace, nonviolence, and social change, such as peace activists groups, peace studies programs, peace newsletters and books, and community peace groups

141 W. Harvey Street
Philadelphia, PA 19144
(215) 849-4941
http://members.aol.com/rasphila/peace.html

Seeds of Peace

Nonprofit, nonpolitical organization that helps teenagers from regions of conflict learn the skills of making peace to equip the next generation with the leadership capabilities required to end the cycles of violence

370 Lexington Avenue, Suite 401
New York, NY 10017
(212) 573-8040
www.seedsofpeace.org

Sierra Club

Grassroots organization that works to explore, enjoy, and protect the wild places of the earth; practice and promote the responsible use of the earth's ecosystems and resources; and educate and enlist humanity to protect and restore the quality of the natural and human environment

85 Second Street, 2nd Floor
San Francisco, CA 94105
(415) 977-5500

www.sierraclub.org

Silent Unity

Nondenominational prayer ministry more than a century old that conducts a twenty-four-hour prayer vigil and daily prayer services

1901 NW Blue Parkway
Unity Village, MO 64065
(816) 524-3550

www.unityworldhq.org

Sounds True

Company that offers video and audio tapes on subjects of spiritual growth and human potential

413 S. Arthur Avenue
Louisville, CO 80027
(800) 333-9185

www.soundstrue.com

THE CARTER CENTER

Organization that works for human rights and the alleviation of human suffering through conflict resolution, enhanced freedom and democracy, and improved health

1762 Clifton Road
Atlanta, GA 30322
(404) 727-7611

www.cartercenter.org

THE EDUCATION FOR PEACE IN IRAQ CENTER (EPIC)

Group that aims to change U.S. foreign policy and raise public awareness in support of human rights in Iraq and peace in the Middle East

1101 Pennsylvania Avenue SE
Washington, DC 20003
(202) 543-6176

www.epic-usa.org

THE FUND FOR PEACE

Organization that works to prevent war and alleviate its causes, through education and research on practical solutions, the promotion of social justice, and respect for democracy

1701 K Street NW, 11th Floor
Washington, DC 20006
(202) 223-7940

www.fundforpeace.org

The Interfaith Alliance

Network that unites more than 150,000 people from more than 50 faith traditions to advance the shared values of compassion, civility, justice, and respect for life

1331 H Street NW, 11th Floor
Washington, DC 20005
(202) 639-6370

www.interfaithalliance.org

The King Center

Living memorial that uses diverse communications media to educate people about the life, work, philosophy, and methods of nonviolent conflict reconciliation and social change advocated by Dr. Martin Luther King, Jr.

449 Auburn Avenue, NE
Atlanta, GA 30312
(404) 526-8900

www.thekingcenter.com

The Masters Group

Group that helps others express their highest potential as a means to enrich relationships and foster the transformation of society, through projects such as the Cloth of Many Colors and a Citizen's Department of Peace

5500 Holmes Run Parkway, Suite 308
Alexandria, VA 22304
(703) 751-7823

www.themastersgroup.org

The Nonviolence Web

Web site that provides up-to-the-minute news and commentary on peace and nonviolence, with links to many related organizations

www.nonviolence.org

The Peace Company

Not-for-profit-only company dedicated to creating a culture of peace through various products, consulting services, and training programs

P.O. Box 253
Bristol, VT 05443
(888) 455-5355

www.thepeacecompany.com

The Shalem Institute for Spiritual Formation

Ecumenical community dedicated to helping mediate God's Spirit in the world through the loving wisdom of contemplative tradition, with programs such as an annual Slow Walk for Peace

5430 Grosvenor Lane
Bethesda, Maryland 20814
(301) 897-7334
www.shalem.org

UNICEF

Permanent part of the United Nations system that helps children living in poverty in developing countries

www.unicef.org

United for Peace and Justice

Collaborative group of national and international peace and social justice organizations, local places of worship, peace centers, and community-based organizations dedicated to peace that tracks issues and events nationwide

www.unitedforpeace.org

United Nations High Commission for Human Rights

Group that documents issues and events related to human rights around the world

www.unhchr.ch

United States Institute of Peace

Independent, nonpartisan federal institution created and funded by Congress to strengthen the nation's capacity to promote the peaceful resolution of international conflicts

www.usip.org

247

Voice4Change

Web site that describes and links to organizations working to improve conditions around the world related to human dignity and justice

www.voice4change.org

WebActive!

Group that uses the Internet and radio broadcasts to provide news and information that supports progressive activism

www.webactive.com

Witness for Peace

Nonviolent, faith-based organization that supports peace, justice, and sustained economies in the Americas

1229 15th Street NW
Washington, DC 20005
(202) 588-1471

www.w4peace.org

Women Against Military Madness

Organization working for local justice and peace

310 East 38th Street, Suite 225
Minneapolis, MN 55409
(612) 827-5364

www.worldwidewamm.org

Women's Actions for New Directions (WAND)

Group that empowers women to act politically to reduce violence and militarism, and to redirect excessive military resources toward unmet human and environmental needs

www.wand.org

World Federalist Association

Nonprofit citizens' organization working for a democratic world federation limited to achieving positive global goals that nations cannot accomplish alone

418 Seventh Street SE
Washington, DC 20003
(800) WFA-0123

www.wfa.org

World Future Society

Nonprofit educational and scientific organization for people interested in how social and technological developments are shaping the future

7910 Woodmont Avenue, Suite 450
Bethesda, MD 20814
(800) 989-8274

www.wfs.org

World Peace Prayer Society

Nonprofit, nonsectarian, member-supported organization dedicated to uniting the hearts of humanity through the universal prayer, *May Peace Prevail on Earth*; sponsor of peace flag and peace pole ceremonies, youth for peace, peace pals, world peace festivals, and the World Peace Sanctuary

26 Benton Road
Wassaic, NY 12592
(845) 877-6093

www.worldpeace.org

World Resources Institute

Environmental think tank that goes beyond research to find practical ways to protect the earth and improve people's lives

10 G Street NE, Suite 800
Washington, DC 20002
(202) 729-7600
www.wri.org

World Wildlife Fund

Largest privately supported international conservation organization in the world, dedicated to protecting the world's wildlife and wild lands

1250 Twenty-Fourth Street NW
P.O. Box 97180
Washington, DC 20090-7180
(800) CALL-WWF
www.worldwildlife.org

251

Worldwatch Institute

Nonprofit public policy research organization dedicated to informing policymakers and the public about emerging global problems and trends and the complex links between the world economy and its environmental support systems

1776 Massachusetts Avenue, NW
Washington, DC 20036-1904
(202) 452-1999
www.worldwatch.org

It's about time we begin it, to turn the world around.
It's about time we start to make it, the dream
  we've always known.
It's about time we start to live it, the family of man.
It's about time, it's about changes, and it's about time.
It's about peace and it's about plenty and it's about time.
It's about you and me together, and it's about time.

– John Denver

Acknowledgments and Attributions

Writing this book was a labor of love, filled with surprising challenges and substantial rewards. Its completion was possible only with help from many dear friends, colleagues, and family members. I am especially grateful to Mary Lou Adams, Liz Clist, Tina Jackson, Krista Kurth, Arleen LaBella, Michael Milano, Brenda Principe, and Suzanne Schmidt for their loving guidance, unwavering encouragement, and willingness to respond to my repeated requests for reviews and suggestions. My wholehearted thanks also go to Mark Tucker, whose inspiringly beautiful photographs amplify the message of peace within these pages. Mark's generosity of spirit and exceptional talent were instrumental in making my dream a reality.

I offer special thanks to Louise Diamond for her kindness and encouragement throughout my writing process, and for her shining example of how to live a life of and for peace. Her foreword to the book mirrors my vision of the requirement for peace in today's world, and the responsibility of each of us to respond to the call, for which I am profoundly grateful.

I also extend my heartfelt gratitude to Rev. Claudell County and Rev. Wilma Donald for the peace meditations they lovingly created, and to Maya Porter, who, in addition to providing expert editing support, helped me continually clarify and stay true to my highest vision for the book. Designers Kyle McKibbin and Kelly Jamison deserve special thanks for making the first and last steps in the publishing process much easier than I expected. Thanks also to Amber Sessler for formatting the book, and to Callie Oettinger for guiding me through a confusing set of tasks on the way to printing.

To my longtime friend Carolann Heckman, whose expert proofreading, persistence, and light-hearted style made possible all those last-minute corrections, I offer an extra "Thank you!" In addition, for their valuable

253

contributions, I gratefully acknowledge Linda Brown, Carole Crumley, Gloria Cousar, Elaine English, Jerry Hampton, Bernette Holland, Donna Montgomery, Ellyn Pollack, Bruce Robinette, Evleen and Eric Sass, Bob Stevens, Lori and Tom Thompson, and Howard Yoon. Each of these supporters added their special touch or energy to the book. And, for their willingness to review and comment on the final product, I express my deep gratitude to Liz Clist, Gordon Davidson, Louise Diamond, James Durst, Stephen Fiske, Carolann Heckman, Ann Kline, Krista Kurth, Judie LaRosa, Michelle Lusson, Michael Milano, Thomas Moore, Robert Rabbin, John Renesch, Bob Rosen, and Suzanne Schmidt.

Ripples of Peace is made richer by the insights and expertise of people whose visions of peace far exceed my own. In adding their wise words, I have made every attempt to abide by the "fair use" stipulation of copyright law and to ensure the accuracy and correct attribution of these quotes. Any errors brought to my attention will be corrected in subsequent printings. The sources of all quotations are listed on the following pages.

Page	*Quotation*	*Source*
xix	Mohandas K. Gandhi	Quoted on Fellowship of Reconciliation web site (*www.forusa.org/Quotes/Gandhi*)
xix	Jawaharlal Nehru	Quoted on *Think Exist* web site (*www.thinkexist.com*)
xx	Sogyal Rinpoche	*Glimpse After Glimpse* by Rinpoche, June 9
2	Lao-Tsu	*Natural Health* magazine, December 2001, p. 90
8	John Wooden	From peace quotes on *John WorldPeace* web site (*www.johnworldpeace.com*)
8	Melodie Beattie	*The Language of Letting Go* by Beattie, p. 218
14	The Buddha	Quoted on *Om Place* web site (*www.omplace.com*)
14	Neville	*The Power of Awareness* by Neville, pp. 10–11

Page	Quotation	Source
182	Native American prayer for peace	Quoted on *Emissary of Light* web site (*www.emissaryoflight.com*)
182	Swami Omkar	*Meditation* by Easwaren, p. 227
183	Paramahansa Yogananda	Quoted in *Prayer* by Dunn, p. 209
183	Frank Borman/Apollo 8	Quoted on *www.msnbc.com/news*
184	Thomas Moore	*Meditations* by Moore, p. 68
194	Albert Einstein	Quoted on *www.musicfolio.com*
194	Congressman Dennis J. Kucinich	Exerpt from "America, A New Spirit, A New Generation of Peace"
200	Peace Pilgrim	Quoted on *Nuclear Age Peace Foundation* web site (*www.wagingpeace.com*)
200	Anne Frank	Quoted on *OmPlace* web site (*www.omplace.com*)
200	Stephen Longfellow Fiske	Excerpt from "Bridges of Love" by Fiske
252	John Denver	Excerpt from "It's About Time" by Denver

About the Author

Rae Thompson is a freelance writer with a passion for peace, conscious communication, and consciousness raising. Since launching her business (Heartswork) in the early 1990s, she has written or collaborated on nearly 50 books, training guides, corporate and government documents, book proposals, and articles. Rae is committed to topics that foster individual awareness, promote organization and community health, and inspire, empower, and uplift the human spirit.

Rae's background includes a B.A. in psychology and graduate work in the social sciences. She has more than thirty years experience in research, program development, strategic planning, management, facilitation, training, and organization development. She founded Heartswork on her belief that widespread change occurs one person at a time and that true transformation begins with each advocate of change. By integrating tools for personal integrity with systems theory and conscious language, Rae partners with others to promote individual and collective transformation through the written word.

For more information on Rae and Heartswork, go to *www.hearts-work.com.*

261

About the Photographer

Mark Tucker is a nationally acclaimed speaker and photographer who has been illuminating the human condition for more than eighteen years. His enchanting and lyrical presentations are inspirational journeys honoring the majesty and wonder of life. More than a half-million people throughout the world have been uplifted and inspired by his photographic works of art.

Mark masterfully blends music and imagery in multi-media slide shows that evoke profound reverence for the sacredness of life. He has been hosted by the U.S. Pentagon; the U.S. Senate and House of Representatives; the United Nations; Harvard, Yale, and Princeton Universities; *National Geographic*; Eastman-Kodak; Chrysler; and Johnson & Johnson—as well as countless numbers of social, spiritual, academic, and health care centers around the globe. His work has drawn praise from Joan Borysenko, Gerald Jampolsky, Bernie Siegel, Ram Dass, and many others.

For more information on Mark and Healing Heart Productions, go to *www.healing-heart.com*.

Sharing Peace

One of the most rewarding experiences I've had writing *Ripples of Peace* is hearing the wonderful ideas of friends and family members inspired by the notion that peace begins with each of us. One friend has started leading discussions on peace in her church. Another friend plans to sell the book to help raise money for her daughter's school, while focusing the students' attention on peace. My cousin is talking about making peace montages with her four boys, ages six to sixteen, who love being creative. And several of my colleagues are developing ways to nurture peace at work.

As I continue to talk with people about ways to create peace in the world, I hear expressions of hope for our future. I see people beginning to tap into their own reservoirs of peace. And I sense their willingness to take actions, however big or small, to create peace in their own lives and to share peace with others.

This eagerness of so many people to make a commitment to peace has prompted me to take another step on my personal path of peace. As *Ripples of Peace* goes to press, I'm getting ready to compile a new book— one filled with ideas and stories from people taking a stand for peace. People like you! And I plan to donate a percentage of the book's proceeds to peace-related organizations.

I invite you to join me in extending our ripples of peace. Please send me your ideas for creating peace and your stories of peace. I'll compile and publish the most inspiring ones in a companion to *Ripples of Peace.*

If sharing peace in this way appeals to you, just follow the guidelines on the next page. Then submit your information on the attached form or on *www.ripples-of-peace.com.*

Your Peace Ideas and Stories

▪ What are your ideas for peace?
Describe what you have done to create and sustain peace for your-self; share peace with family and friends; or promote peace within your community, nation, and the world.

▪ What are your stories of peace?
Describe your personal experiences with one or more of the ideas in *Ripples of Peace*, or with other ways you have created peace in your life.

▪ How have you raised funds for your organization?
Describe how you have used *Ripples of Peace* or other products and projects to raise funds for your community, place of worship, school, or peace-related organization.

Feel free to send in more than one idea or story. Be sure to include your contact information so I can verify or clarify material selected for publication, and notify you when the new book is published.

Blessings and peace,

Rae Thompson

To order additional copies of *Ripple of Peace: 111 Ways You Can Help Create Peace in the World*, log on to *www.ripples-of-peace.com* or call Heartswork Publications, 703-648-1464.

Check out the special discount for bulk purchases!

TO: Heartswork Publications
2169 Glencourse Lane
Reston, VA 20191–1345

FROM: (*All* items are required. Please *print* clearly.)

Name _____

Address _____

_____

_____

Phone _____

E-mail _____

Dear Rae:

Here is my personal idea or story about peace. Please review it for possible inclusion in the companion book to *Ripples of Peace*. I affirm that it is true and accurate and give you permission to use my name in your book. I also give you permission to contact me to clarify information and edits, and to notify me of the book's publication.

Signature _____ Date _____

PEACE IDEA OR STORY: (Add pages as necessary.)